UNMASKING
THE POWER
OF THE SCOUTS

GAINING INTEL FOR VICTORY
OVER YOUR OPPOSITION

Book Synopsis

Are you tired of unnecessary warfare and burnout due to demonic contention? Do you need your prayer life and prayer team to SHIFT dimensions to adequately cover you so you can advance the kingdom of God without constant demonic interferences? Do you need revelation and activation about entering realms and scouting out demonic activity so you can be offensive against the enemy? Do you desire heavenly prayer revelation that equips you for the people, platform, regions, and territories that God has assigned to you? Learn all of this and more in this groundbreaking book.

UNMASKING THE POWER OF THE SCOUTS
Volume I: Gaining Intel For Victory Over Your Opposition

Kingdomshifterscec@gmail.com
www.kingdomshifters.com
Connect with Taquetta via Facebook or YouTube

Contents

Taquetta's Story (abridged edition)

Taquetta was adopted by her aunt at two weeks old. She was raised with four brothers in East St. Louis and has been a fighter since she was a little girl. God has transformed that fighting personality into a spiritual warrior in his kingdom! She has a testimony of having her fists turned into hands of prayer, complete with a gift of healing and faith for miracles, signs, and wonders to manifest. God transformed Taquetta from one who frequented nightclubs and battled alcoholism to one with a strategy to empower others in destiny. Her name means "child of love," and she carries that mantle by loving others. Taquetta is gifted at empowering and assisting people with launching ministries, businesses, and books. She provides mentoring, counseling and destiny development through Kingdom Shifters Kingdom Wellness Program. She is a gourmet cook, loves to shop, and is a serious fan of *The Golden Girls*. Her door is always open to welcome others to rest in her gift of hospitality.

Taquetta flows through the wells of warfare and worship. She carries the mantle, not only of her spiritual mother, Dr. Kathy Williams, but also of her overseer and apostolic mother, Dr. Jackie Green. Her mantle includes an apostolic mandate of judging and establishing God's kingdom in people, ministries, communities, and regions. Taquetta travels in foreign missions and throughout the United States. She has mentored and established dance, altar workers, deliverance, and prophetic ministries. Taquetta ministers in the areas of fine arts, all manners of prayer, fivefold ministry, deliverance, healing, miracles, atmospheric worship, and empowers and train people in their destiny and life vision. She walks the walk and rejoices at the expansion of God's kingdom!

Taquetta's Credentials

- Founder of Kingdom Shifters Ministries (KSM), Indiana and Kingdom Shifters Empowerment Church, Virginia
- Founder of Kingdom Wellness Counseling and Mentoring Center
- Author of over 38 books and 2 prayer decree CD's
- Doctorate in Ministry from Rapha Deliverance University
- Master's Degree in Community Counseling with an emphasis on Marriage, Children and Family Counseling
- Bachelor's Degree in Psychology
- Associates Degree in Business Administration
- Therapon Belief Therapist Certification from the Therapon Institute (faith-based counseling)
- Board of Directors for New Day Community Ministries, Inc.
- Graduate of Eagles Dance Institute under Dr. Pamela Hardy; licensed in the area of liturgical dance
- Apostolic Ordination by Bishop Jackie Green, Founder of JGM-National Prayer Life Institute (Phoenix, AZ)
- Previous ministry service as prophet, visionary for Shekinah Expressions Dance Troupe, teacher, member of presbytery, overseer for altar workers' ministry

FOREWORD – Dr. Jackie Green

It is time for the Body of Christ to grow up and not only have dominion in the earth, but "strategically stand" against the *spiritual spheres* in the darkness and sit in the heavenly places." The Church has been laid back in the deep things of God, and just "marked time" for too long. This book is an invitation to a crucial area of spiritual warfare, Unmasking the Power of the Scouts" Volume One, that has been neglected area because many church leaders lack the spiritual discipline and revelation to teach these strategic "Scouting" principles. Not often do I get to sit a read a fresh new book in one sitting. This book will captivate the Watchman and yes, the Scout. You will not be able to put it down until you have eaten it all.

I've been waiting for Apostle Taquetta to press through and birth this book since she first mentioned that she was working on it. It has blessed me and strengthened me from the mundane and draining church routines in warfare one can get stuck in. It is a fresh approach to high level warfare for anyone willing to pay the price in time, travail, obedience to the Holy Spirit, and teaching and leading us into new levels and Kingdom intelligence.

Having been on the front lines of national and international warfare, governmental spheres and church warfare since 1983, some 37 years, I don't feel no ways tired, and yet I am still learning and growing. It's a no-nonsense tool as we enter the 21st century. Apostle Taquetta, a Millennial apostle and prophet, continues to amaze us and challenge us where we've been and where we should be going in the spiritual realms. *There is an invisible yet visible "spiritual intelligence realm" of war going on in the heavenly realms that we must quickly get in place for.* This war is above and over our heads in high places, and not with one another.

This book will help the Body of Christ *"come up hither"* and gather the intelligence we need from the Holy Spirit and from *Holy Scouts* sent by the Lord into high places. We can no longer allow the enemy scouts to sift information and have access and demonic data over us. We must be wiser and have greater discernment in the Holy Ghost.

I love Dr. Baker's concept of the "Night Scout," for I love night and night warfare because God made the night, and when He made it, He called it good. The Church has allowed the Devil to rule the night too long. We must regain those lost territories of souls and take the Night back! The Body of Christ cannot sleep through the night warfare. This is where the scouts, the "NIGHT SCOUT" must arise, be equipped and available to carry out the night watchman assignments.

Dr. Baker defines the SCOUT as, *"A scout operates in the offensive positions of a watchman, seer, prophets, dreamer, intercessor, soldier, stealth bomber, and sniper. Scouts are employed to inspect, observe, or survey the enemy in order to gain and gather information for military purposes.* It is not until you have encountered the spiritual real with dark forces and heavenly forces and attacks on our dream realms that you realize there is more to life than going to church every Sunday. There are "Scouting" positions available in the Kingdom of God that have been vacant for a long season.

Finally, I concur with this entire treatise how to Unmask The Power Of The Scout. I was particularly stirred with the definitions on "Side Lash" and "Petty Lash." I have experienced many of the demonic lashes against my life and family, our ministry teams and churches. This book is crucial training for the "expert watchman." We can be experts because Christ is our Lord over all and His Holy Spirit within the Saints is All-knowing.

We don't have a lot of time to waste, so this book will get *the Scouts enlisted,* equipped and empowered for the great spiritual warfare presently and in the future. Thank you Apostle Taquetta for the hours and hours of intercession, scribing, boldness and breakthrough that will come from this kingdom *"Spiritual Intelligence" Handbook.*

Blessings,
Bishop Dr. Jackie L. Green, Founder/Overseer
JGM Enternational PrayerLife Institute, Redlands, California

FOREWORD – Prophet Teshania Blackwell

Unmasking the Power of the Scout…WHEW!! Where do I even begin? This magnificently scripted work is undeniably anointed and something everyone who is called to be an intercessor or armorbearer should read, digest, meditate on and apply. It is then, you will witness the transformation you will experience, not just in your prayer life, but in every area of your life. Why? Because in order to understand and walk in the POWER of the SCOUT, your mindset must and will SHIFT after surveying through this wealth of wisdom, knowledge and revelation concerning the scout.

Dr. Taquetta Baker skillfully breaks down the definition, responsibilities, accountability and duties of a scout, as a surgeon outlining to her colleagues the procedures of a surgery. The keen insight and depth to which she explains this topic is surely what is needed for all who walk as scouts or watchmen for a person, ministry, business, organization or region.

Reading this book caused me to look back on times that I was blessed, privileged and honored to serve great generals in the Kingdom. First, the late great Bishop John H. Boyd Sr. at New Greater Bethel Ministries and then the prophet to the nations, Dr. Juanita Bynum. I remember before even serving Bishop Boyd in the capacity of an armorbearer (at the time I didn't even understand what that even was!), I expressed to the Lord my desire to see what was going on in the enemies camp so I could be proactive in my prayer and actions. It was my thought that understanding the heavenly things of God, i.e. angelic hosts, will only assist us as believers and not harm us. However, we must understand the adversary's plans and what is going on in his camp because the adversary desires to snuff out the believer. Essentially, I was referring to operating as a SCOUT! I just didn't have a term for it. I just knew it needed to be done. Additionally, I remember expressing this to a seasoned saint about seeing into the enemy's camp, and she looked at me and said, "No baby, you don't want to do that." My reply, was simply, "yes I do want to do that." Otherwise, how can you get ahead and stop him at his own game?

Moreover, when I began the awesome assignment of armorbearing, interceding for Dr. Juanita Bynum before, during, and after she delivered the word, I now see a great deal of the details the Holy Spirit taught me, are within the pages of this book. Without a doubt, as Dr. Taquetta states in this book, "you must know what you are walking into in order to be preemptive." It is advantageous to know what the strongholds are in the region, the history, culture, the patterns etc. Also, within the pages of this book, Dr. Taquetta Baker explains the revelation of the scout in a manner that is easy to understand, digest and implement.

From spirits that attack ministers to demonic collaboration among regions better known as demonic confederacy and beyond, this book is dynamic. Dr. Taquetta has nailed it. This piece of written work is dynamic in every aspect. It without a doubt, exposes the tactics of the enemy and reminds the believer of the supernatural power that is available within us, because of the work of the cross, to defeat and outmaneuver our adversary. This book is full of rich instructions pertaining to spiritual warfare and is certainly a sound piece of written work which has a biblical basis for all that has been presented within these pages.

Dr. Taquetta Baker has included prayers to cover ministers, event covering, spiritual mapping and so much more. If you already have or intend to develop an intercessory team or armorbearing team, do yourself a favor and make this a required reading. I have watched Dr. Taquetta Baker and observed, when she did not even know it. She has developed into a woman of God who walks the talk and is fierce and fearless when it comes to comprehending infiltration of the adversary's camp and getting intel to destroy the darkness, thus thwarting the plan of the enemy. Dr. Taquetta Baker is what I would call an authority in this realm and was assuredly born to birth this. She is passionate about destroying the kingdom of darkness and is even more so about believers understanding the authority they walk in and using it efficiently and adeptly for victorious living.

Dr. Taquetta Baker truly is a force to be reckoned with and is credentialed spiritually and naturally. She is God's woman, infused with character and integrity; blazing trails for others to follow. As believers, intercessors, armorbearers, deliverance ministers, etc., you will become galvanized to walk in your authority. Inasmuch as you read this book and is guided by the Holy Spirit, you will especially, understand the necessity of Unmasking the Power of the Scout!

Blessings,
Prophet Teshania Blackwell
Founder of "The Visionary" Ministries, Newark, Delaware

All POWER & AUTHORITY TO CAST OUT

This chapter is intended to stir your authority so that as you SHIFT into the rest of this manual, you will advance inside the truth that you have all dominion over every demon, all unrighteousness and evil manner in the earth. As scouts, we must embody this TRUTH and assert our kingly right to cast out, annihilate, and overthrow every demonic entity of witchcraft, demonology, lawlessness, and wickedness. For Jesus commissioned us to:

Matthew 10:8 Heal the sick, cleanse the lepers, raise the dead, cast out devils: freely ye have received, freely give.

Mark 16:17-18 And these signs shall follow them that believe; In my name shall they cast out devils; they shall speak with new tongues; They shall take up serpents; and if they drink any deadly thing, it shall not hurt them; they shall lay hands on the sick, and they shall recover.

<u>*Cast Out*</u> is *ekballō* in Greek and means:
- to eject (literally or figuratively)
- bring forth, cast (forth, out), drive (out)
- expel, leave, pluck (pull, take, thrust) out
- put forth (out), send away (forth, out)
- cast out, cast, bring forth, pull out, send forth, send out
- drive out, to send out with notion of violence
- to cast out a.of the world, i.e., be deprived of the power and influence he exercises in the world
- a thing: excrement from the belly into the sink
- to expel a person from a society, to banish from a family
- to compel one to depart; to bid one depart, in stern though not violent language
- so employed that the rapid motion of the one going is transferred to the one sending forth
- to command or cause one to depart in haste

1

- to draw out with force
- tear out with implication of force overcoming opposite force a.to cause a thing to move straight on its intended goal
- to reject with contempt, to cast off or away
- to draw out, extract, one thing inserted in another
- to bring out of, to draw or bring forth
- to except, to leave out, i.e. not receive
- to lead one forth or away somewhere with a force which he cannot resist

Dictionary.com defines *cast* as:

Throw aside	Cast	Eject	Expel	Heave	Hurl	Launch
Expulsion	Fling	Pitch	Project	Shoot	Sling	Thrust
Toss	Drive	Discharge	Excrete	Eliminate	End	Terminate

As scouts, we should not allow demons to cohabitate, negotiate, compromise, live, govern or rule in our lives, families, generational lines, homes, lands, regions, spheres, ministries, business, organizations, destinies, visions and callings. The kingdom should be our portion on earth as it is in heaven.

Matthew 28:18-19 And Jesus came and spake unto them, saying, All power is given unto me in heaven and in earth. Go ye therefore, and teach all nations, baptizing them in the name of the Father, and of the Son, and of the Holy Ghost

The Message Bible Verse 18-20 Jesus, undeterred, went right ahead and gave his charge: "God authorized and commanded me to commission you: Go out and train everyone you meet, far and near, in this way of life, marking them by baptism in the threefold name: Father, Son, and Holy Spirit. Then instruct them in the practice of all I have commanded you. I'll be with you as you do this, day after day after day, right up to the end of the age."

Jesus was given two distinct dimensions of authority – heaven and earth. This authority was preeminent – supreme. It was nonnegotiable! It was the highest honor bestowed upon him as ruling savior who demonstrated with his very being that he embodied the eternal sovereign power of God.

He then SHIFTED that authority on to us. It is now a part of our identity as his disciples and laborers in the earth.

Ephesians 1:17-23 New International Bible I keep asking that the God of our Lord Jesus Christ, the glorious Father, may give you the Spirit of wisdom and revelation, so that you may know him better. I pray that the eyes of your heart may be enlightened in order that you may know the hope to which he has called you, the riches of his glorious inheritance in his holy people, and his incomparably great power for us who believe. That power is the same as the mighty strength he exerted when he raised Christ from the dead and seated him at his right hand in the heavenly realms, far above all rule and authority, power and dominion, and every name that is invoked, not only in the present age but also in the one to come. And God placed all things under his feet and appointed him to be head over everything for the church, which is his body, the fullness of him who fills everything in every way.

In this passage, Paul was praying that the believers would gain insight of this authority through the purposes and works of the cross. That such comprehension would SHIFT them into greater knowledge, revelation, understanding, intimacy and covenant with Jesus. Paul reveals that this is a part of our God identity and kingly inheritance as sons of God and shared laborers in the faith. We must take our rightful place in sonship. We must assert our right to govern in both realms, live in heavenly realms, while utilizing our destinies and callings, and scouting authority to SHIFT heaven to earth. When we fail to do this, demons and demonic systems takeover our spheres of influence and produce their sinful, destructive kingdom purposes in our midst.

I decree that as you study the scripture below, you receive an impartation of the truth that you have ALL POWER OVER ALL

THE POWER OF THE ENEMY! I decree a fierce, bold, Jesus death defying anointing embodies you where you fear nothing but Jesus.

Matthew 4:10 Then Jesus said to him, "Go, Satan! For it is written, 'YOU SHALL WORSHIP THE LORD YOUR GOD, AND SERVE HIM ONLY.'"

Luke 11:14 And He was casting out a demon, and it was mute; when the demon had gone out, the mute man spoke; and the crowds were amazed.

Matthew 8:16 When evening came, they brought to Him many who were demon-possessed; and He cast out the spirits with a word, and healed all who were ill.

Mark 1:34 And He healed many who were ill with various diseases, and cast out many demons; and He was not permitting the demons to speak, because they knew who He was.

Luke 4:41 Demons also were coming out of many, shouting, "You are the Son of God!" But rebuking them, He would not allow them to speak, because they knew Him to be the Christ.

Mark 1:39 And He went into their synagogues throughout all Galilee, preaching and casting out the demons.

Luke 13:32 And He said to them, "Go and tell that fox, 'Behold, I cast out demons and perform cures today and tomorrow, and the third day I reach My goal.'

Luke 4:35 But Jesus rebuked him, saying, "Be quiet and come out of him!" And when the demon had thrown him down in the midst of the people, he came out of him without doing him any harm.

Matthew 8:32 And He said to them, "Go!" And they came out and went into the swine, and the whole herd rushed down the steep bank into the sea and perished in the waters.

Mark 5:8 For He had been saying to him, "Come out of the man, you unclean spirit!"

Luke 8:29 For He had commanded the unclean spirit to come out of the man. For it had seized him many times; and he was bound with chains and shackles and kept under guard, and yet he would break his bonds and be driven by the demon into the desert.

Mark 9:25 When Jesus saw that a crowd was rapidly gathering, He rebuked the unclean spirit, saying to it, "You deaf and mute spirit, I command you, come out of him and do not enter him again."

Mark 7:26 Now the woman was a Gentile, of the Syrophoenician race. And she kept asking Him to cast the demon out of her daughter.

Matthew 8:31 The demons began to entreat Him, saying, "If You are going to cast us out, send us into the herd of swine."

Matthew 9:33 After the demon was cast out, the mute man spoke; and the crowds were amazed, and were saying, "Nothing like this has ever been seen in Israel."

Mark 16:9 [Now after He had risen early on the first day of the week, He first appeared to Mary Magdalene, from whom He had cast out seven demons.

Matthew 9:34 But the Pharisees were saying, "He casts out the demons by the ruler of the demons."

Matthew 12:24 But when the Pharisees heard this, they said, "This man casts out demons only by Beelzebul the ruler of the demons."

Matthew 12:27 If I by Beelzebul cast out demons, by whom do your sons cast them out? For this reason they will be your judges.

Mark 3:22 The scribes who came down from Jerusalem were saying, "He is possessed by Beelzebul," and "He casts out the demons by the ruler of the demons."

Luke 11:15 But some of them said, "He casts out demons by Beelzebul, the ruler of the demons."

Luke 11:18-19 If Satan also is divided against himself, how will his kingdom stand? For you say that I cast out demons by Beelzebul. "And if I by Beelzebul cast out demons, by whom do your sons cast them out? So they will be your judges.

Matthew 12:26 If Satan casts out Satan, he is divided against himself; how then will his kingdom stand?

Luke 11:20 But if I cast out demons by the finger of God, then the kingdom of God has come upon you.

Matthew 12:28 But if I cast out demons by the Spirit of God, then the kingdom of God has come upon you.

ANOINTED OPERATIONS OF A SCOUT

When you are called as an intercessory watchman for a person, ministry, business, organization, or region, you are serving in the position of a scout.

A scout operates in the offensive positions of a watchman, seer, prophets, dreamer, intercessor, soldier, stealth bomber, and sniper. Scouts are employed to inspect, observe, or survey the enemy in order to gain and gather information for military purposes. You observe and report on the following:

- Their character, nature, and personality,
- Abilities and capabilities,
- Likes and dislikes,
- Habits and patterns,
- Strengths and weaknesses,
- Movements, locations, and operations,
- Strategies and techniques,
- Environments and habitats to which they maneuver and dwell,
- Their identity, purpose, and mission,
- Their personal, geographical, and generational power and operation,
- History, culture, language and communication strategies.

Your intel is beneficial to being offensive against the enemy, while annihilating any present or future plan of attack or counterattack.

A scout is the eyes and ears for the army of the Lord. When intel is needed on the enemy, you can maneuver around the enemy's camp or on the battle ground and collect intel.

"A scout is the eyes and ears for the army of the Lord.

Scouts are not meant to be seen and are not trying to be seen. If you have a need to be seen, then you are not a scout. A need to be seen will result in you and your team attacked.

If a scout can be seen it is because God is allowing it and has called the scout to continuously confront the powers of darkness with their presence. A scout with this mandate will have constant opposition with the powers of darkness for the purposes of being God's judgment, justice, authority, exposer, and annihilator of darkness everywhere that they go.

Scouts are fearless and can detect the salvation of the Lord in a situation. No matter what they observe, they maintain the eyes, ears, goodness, and victories of God. If you are a scaredy cat and are swayed by your emotions, circumstances, and the powers of your enemy then you are yet ready to operate as a scout. At minimum, you need a qualified mentor who will help you develop in your calling. It is not yet time for you to be active in the role of a scout. Scouts always know God is greater than anything and that they are greater through him.

Scouts encourage others to see God's hand in a situation or to see a situation like God sees it.

Scouts are self-sacrificing to the cause, good of the vision, and the people.

Scouts operate under a stealth bomber and a sniper anointing.

Stealth Bomber - A stealth bomber is one who maneuvers into the enemy's camp undetected to save people, recover things that have been stolen, combat the enemy, destroy spiritual covens and high places, etc.

Psalms 18:28-29 For thou wilt light my candle: the Lord my God will enlighten my darkness. For by thee I have run through a troop; and by my God have I leaped over a wall.

Sniper – enters the spirit realm undetected while blending, hiding, and moving about strategically to gain intel and attack the enemy.

Joshua 23:10 One man of you shall chase a thousand: for the Lord your God, he it is that fighteth for you, as he hath promised you.

Chase (*radap*) in this scripture means, *"to pursue, hunt, attend closely to, persecute, put to flight."* A scout possesses capabilities to discern their target, gain intel, and annihilate the enemy.

In the Old Testament, scouting was used as a warfare tactic. Moses and Joshua sent men to scout out the land.

Deuteronomy 1:22 Then all of you approached me and said, 'Let us send men before us, that they may search out the land for us, and bring back to us word of the way by which we should go up and the cities which we shall enter.'

Numbers 13:1-2 And the Lord spoke to Moses, saying, "Send men to spy out the land of Canaan, which I am giving to the children of Israel; from each tribe of their fathers you shall send a man, every one a leader among them."

Joshua 7:2 New International Bible Joshua sent some of his men from Jericho to spy out the town of Ai, east of Bethel, near Beth-aven.

In the New Testament, scouting was used as a tactic to seize Jesus with intent of crucifying him and to spy on the disciples.

Luke 20:20-22 So they watched Him, and sent spies who pretended to be righteous, in order that they might catch Him in some statement, so that they could deliver Him to the rule and the authority of the governor. They questioned Him, saying, "Teacher, we know that You speak and teach correctly, and You are not partial to any, but teach the way of God in truth." Is it lawful for us to pay taxes to Caesar, or not?"

Galatians 2:3-5 The Message Bible Significantly, Titus, non-Jewish though he was, was not required to be circumcised. While we were in conference, we were infiltrated by spies pretending to be Christians, who slipped in to find out just how free true Christians are. Their ulterior motive was to reduce us to their brand of servitude. We didn't give them the time of day. We were determined to preserve the truth of the Message for you.

POWER & AUTHORITY OF A SCOUT

The devil roams about as a scout spying out people and the land seeking whom he can devour and sends demons to spy on us.

1Peter 5:8 Be sober, be vigilant; because your adversary the devil, as a roaring lion, walketh about, seeking whom he may devour:

Scouts are called to understand, know, and contend against wiles of devil and his high-ranking demonic forces and powers.

Ephesians 6:12 For we wrestle not against flesh and blood, but against principalities, against powers, against the rulers of the darkness of this world, against spiritual wickedness in high places.

Scouts understand rankings and operate in levels of warfare.

Levels of Warfare

Ground Level Warfare involves casting demons out of individuals, places, and things.

Occult Level Warfare involves witchcraft, idolatry, or strategic organizations that are really powers of darkness, or spiritual wickedness in high places within a community or region. Examples, Freemasonry, Sororities, Fraternities, New Age Practices, Buddhism, Tibetan, Yoga, etc.

Strategic Level Warfare is where principalities and territorial spirits are assigned by Satan to directly bind, influence, and govern the activities of communities, regions, states, and nations. They also coordinate demonic activities in political, governmental, economic, financial, educational, business, and entertainment arenas.

Scouts understand rankings and operate in levels of warfare.

Demon Rankings

Demons are demonic forces, evil spirits or devils that possess, depress, oppress, torment, influence, or stronghold a person, place, or thing. The way these demonic spirits attack is as follows:

- **Oppress** -to burden, restrain, weigh heavy upon, to put down; press down, subdue or suppress an atmosphere or the soul, heart, or body of a person.
- **Depress** – to make sad or gloomy; lower in spirits; deject, dispirit, to lower in force, vigor, activity, etc.; weaken, make dull, a person or atmosphere.
- **Negatively influence**_– cause confusion, discombobulation, double mindedness, unexplainable weariness, tiredness or sluggardness, irritation, frustration, ungodly thoughts, thought racing within a person or atmosphere.
- **Possess** – to occupy, dominate, or control a person or atmosphere.

Strongholds are demonically possessed, demonically depressed, demonically gripping clutches, barriers, fortresses, walls, or entanglements that harass, influence, hinder and/or prevent a person from being free to walk in the full salvation of the Lord (_2 Corinthians 10:3-5, Ephesians 4:22-23, Matthew 16:19, Mark 3:27_).

Principalities are satanic princes and territorial spirits ruling over a nation, city, region, and community for the purposes of establishing Satan's demonic plan in people's lives and spheres.
Powers are high ranking supernatural demons or demonic influences that cause evil and sin in the world.
Rulers of Darkness are demonic forces that govern deception and manipulative hardships and catastrophes that are generally produced by witchcraft, manipulation of the weather and worldly systems; they operate in cultures and countries such that idolatry and sin reign in the earth.

Spiritual Wickedness in High Places are evil plots and deceptions, and demonic attacks directed in and against the church and God's people for the purposes of hindering, contaminating and demolishing God's will in the earth.

Witchcraft Practices

Witchcraft is the practice of magic, especially black magic; it is the utilization of spells and the invocation of demons to bind people, families, ministries, businesses, organizations, land, atmospheres, climates, regions, and nations. Some people engage in witchcraft for entertainment, curiosity, or due to ignorance. Those that dedicate their lives to it use it to acquire personal success and advancement, power, fame, rank in spiritual realms, spheres, and to obtain high ranking positions and platforms in the natural.

As scouts, it is important to study witchcraft and gain intel on their operations. One of your mandates as a scout is to deal with spiritual wickedness in high places and to pull down high places. Witchcraft has become more prevalent and blatant and confrontation of witches, warlocks, and witchcraft is essential for cleansing the land and airways of regions, and dispelling spells sent about the ministers, ministries, organizations and businesses of God.

Witches are known to come to services posing as saints, while releasing spells against the people and purposes of God. They are known to cast spells on ministers and against events. As a scout, you may even encounter witches in your dream realm, during Holy Spirit translations, or during intercessory and spiritual warfare. Scouts are not afraid of witches and witchcraft. Know your authority and gain intel on how witchcraft operates so you can quickly discern and dispel its workings.

Some witchcraft practices include:

Sorcery	Magic	Witching	Wizardry

Black Magic	White Magic	Candle Magic	Spells
Hexes	Vexes	Hoodoo	Voodoo
Wicca	Mojo	Chants	Demonic Crossroads
Santeria	Yoruba Religion	Hinduism	New Age Practices
Horoscopes	Tarot Readings	Psychic Readings	Chain Letters
Familiar Spirits	Spirit Guides	High Priest/Priestess	Demonic Omens
Necromancy	Yoga	Shamanism	Fortune Telling
Hypnotism	Acupuncture	Psychic Powers	Superstition
Reincarnation	Ouija Boards	Fengshai	Good Luck Charms
Buddhism	Tibetan	Freemasonry	Eastern Stars
Sororities/Fraternities	Psychic Readings	Witchery	Pagan Holidays
Chakras	Kundalini	Astrology	Tarot Cards
Numerology	Dream Catchers	Palm Readings	Fortune Cookies
Leylines	Incantations	Psychological Warfare	Demonic Crossroads/Spirits of the Crossroads

Scouts have a strong gift of discernment.

1Corinthians 12:10 mentions the gift of discernment of spirits. Discernment is the ability to "yield a judicial estimation, distinguish, judge, dispute or discern between good and evil, particularly demonic forces."

As a scout, I generally spy out the land, and sometimes I engage the enemy in the field, while tracking and reporting their activity, scouting out their weaponry, locations, conditions, plans, assignments, etc. and report this information to leaders, ministries, intercessory teams, etc.

Sometimes I combat principalities and powers and sometimes the Lord will just have me give this information to people, leaders, and ministries so they can further explore strategies and plans for demolishing demonic kingdoms and covens in their spheres.

Most believers and leaders do not use the information because they do not have this level of discernment or spiritual enlightenment, or they think one or two prayers will be enough. Often, it is God revealing mysteries to bring great victory and blessings that most saints do not want to do the work to obtain. **Kingdom mysteries are vital to the life of a scout.**

Matthew 13:11 He answered and said unto them, because it is given unto you to know the mysteries of the kingdom of heaven, but to them it is not given.

Luke 8:10 He replied, "The knowledge of the mysteries of the kingdom of God has been given to you, but to others I speak in parables, so that, 'Though seeing, they may not see; though hearing, they may not understand.'

1Corinthians 2:12 But God has revealed it to us by the Spirit. The Spirit searches all things, even the deep things of God.

Colossians 1:27 to whom God has chosen to make known among the Gentiles the glorious riches of this mystery, which is Christ in you, the hope of glory.

As a scout, you should be asking for kingdom mysteries as that is where your strategies reside for breakthrough. My ministry is in a very idolatrous and witchcraft territory. Using strategies derived from scouting through mysteries of God has enabled us to annihilate principalities and powers of the enemy and avoid a lot of struggles and hardships that many ministries in our region experience.
As God increases your discernment, the eyes of your understanding are heightened and enlightened with glory to discern the darkness and tactics of devils and wickedness in your sphere and the spheres to which you are scouting.

Ephesians 1:18 The eyes of your understanding being enlightened; that ye may know what is the hope of his calling, and what the riches of the glory of his inheritance in the saints.

The eyes of your understanding are enlightened by:

Seer Vision – God will allow the eyes of your imagination and understanding to be open and empowered so you can peer into someone's life, ministry, business, situation, or region, so you can see what is or will occur. He may give you pictures, images, play by play, a spiritual tour, or full visions. God guides you in this. You do not open this portal yourself as then you have exposed yourself to what is called a "third eye" where you are receiving information illegally and through demonic assistance. The eyes of your understanding are a part of your spirit and thus what is being filtered into your imagination is from God's spirit to your spirit.

Some people see because they have the gift of a seer. Some can pray fiercely in the spirit for a significant length of time, then meditate on the Lord until he opens their understanding and imagination. If you do not flow in this area, then God may use you in other ways. You can also ask God to open your seer vision. Be cognizant of anything you have spoken over your eyes or gifts when God has shown you things and break those curses as they can block your seer gift. Be mindful that what you may see will not always be pretty and heavenly. I see in both realms – the demonic realm and the heavenly realms. Sometimes the demonic realm, covens, high places, and spirit realms are horrifying and appalling. Make sure you are ready to truly see and have dealt with the spirits of fear before asking for this gift. God is not releasing you to share everything you see. People do not always need to know that you see a demon on their head or in their home. What God speaks to you is confidential so you should not be sharing it when that is not part of your assignment. Many people know I see in both realms, so they sometimes want to know what I see. I only share as God leads; otherwise, I become a god to them. That is the most toxic level of idolatry. Ultimately, God is revealing his secrets and mysteries to me as his friend. **Friends do not spill the beans.**

Friends guard and protect what they share with one another. If you say you are called to pray for someone, then you guard and protect them at all cost. You do not take what God shows you and expose them to people and to the enemy.

Dreams & The Sleep Realm – We must understand that our dreams and night season involve real realms. Our body sleeps, but our spirit is eternal and never sleeps. Our spirit can engage God, heaven, spiritual realms, and if exposed, can even be subject to the

---

Friends do not spill the beans.

---

enemy. This is the reason David says in Psalms 91 that he dwells in the secret place of the most high. He understood the potential to engage the enemy while sleep.

God loves to release intel via dreams and dream realms. It is important for scouts not to discount nightmarish type dreams as God could very well be revealing detail. I personally journal all my dreams because even if the enemy caused me to have a nightmare, I make him regret it by examining his operations and exposing the ways he manifested in the dream. I use that information against him by exposing his camp, systems, and operations, which is the reason why he does not attack me in this way anymore. God may sometimes translate (supernatural transport) you in a dream or even just engage you through your spirit as you sleep to deal with principalities and powers. In some cases, it is to gain intel regarding a person or matter you are praying for. God may give you a dream to reveal principalities and powers or how the enemy is attacking or plans to attack. God will give warning dreams to help avoid attacks or reveal keys and strategies and dreams to annihilate the attacks of the enemy. Did you know that the United States had intel that Japan was going to attack Pearl Harbor but those who were in leadership discounted the idea as too outrageous to believe the reports? Do **NOT** make the mistake of dismissing what God shows to you in your dreams.

Scouting is part of my mantle, so as I am going to bed, I ask for prophetic dreams, and divine encounters with the Lord. I use the blood of Jesus and the glory of the Lord to cleanse myself of the day and to surrender anything that would be a hinderance to engaging God and heaven. I command my spirit man to remember my dreams and cancel any attacks from zapping, blocking, and thieving spirits from stealing my dreams. I may ask for a specific dream as it relates to who or what I am praying for or just be open to whatever God wants to download to me. I am very mindful to govern my dreams by getting up and journaling what he is showing to me and taking time to pray so I can acquire the wisdom and revelation mysteries God is revealing. Do not ask for dreams if you are not going to be accountable to governing over them. If you do not have the willingness, then let God speak to you when you are awake and leave the dream realm to those who desire nightly communion with the Lord.

Mind of Christ – As we seek to possess the mind of Christ, he will give us his thoughts, insights, wisdom, revelations, knowledge, counsel, understandings and instructions. We think like he thinks and possess his ability to engage a matter through his intellect.

Philippians 2:5 Let this mind be in you, which was also in Christ Jesus.

1Corinthians 2:13-16 Which things also we speak, not in the words which man's wisdom teacheth, but which the Holy Ghost teacheth; comparing spiritual things with spiritual. But the natural man receiveth not the things of the Spirit of God: for they are foolishness unto him: neither can he know them, because they are spiritually discerned. But he that is spiritual judgeth all things, yet he himself is judged of no man. For who hath known the mind of the Lord, that he may instruct him? But we have the mind of Christ.

Romans 12:2 And be not conformed to this world: but be ye transformed by the renewing of your mind, that ye may prove what is that good, and acceptable, and perfect, will of God.

Sevenfold Spirit of The Lord – God will reveal mysteries through his spirit.

Isaiah 11:2 And the spirit of the Lord shall rest upon him, the spirit of wisdom and understanding, the spirit of counsel and might, the spirit of knowledge and of the fear of the Lord.

John 16:13 Howbeit when he, the Spirit of truth, is come, he will guide you into all truth: for he shall not speak of himself; but whatsoever he shall hear, that shall he speak: and he will shew you things to come.

Knower - God speaks through our knowing. This is when you "just know" wisdoms, truths, standards, rights and wrongs, character and nature, God's will without having any emotions, physical signs, confirmation from any outside force. The sense of "knowing" is not the same as discernment. God created us so his knower is in us.

Romans 1:19-21 The Amplified Bible For that which is known about God is evident to them and made plain in their inner consciousness, because God [Himself] has shown it to them. For ever since the creation of the world His invisible nature and attributes, that is, His eternal power and divinity, have been made intelligible and clearly discernible in and through the things that have been made (His handiworks). So [men] are without excuse [altogether without any defense or justification], Because when they knew and recognized Him as God, they did not honor and glorify Him as God or give Him thanks. But instead they became futile and godless in their thinking [with vain imaginings, foolish reasoning, and stupid speculations] and their senseless minds were darkened.

There are things we will just know about God because he put it in us to know him and to know them. We can reject them, but we know them regardless. We can choose our own will be we know his will regardless. We can become reprobate to them and even deject the outward manifestations of God, but we know regardless.

Many mistake this for intuition (keen and quick insight) or Deja vu (tedious familiarity, feeling of having already experienced the present situation). These tend to operate through our minds, emotions or natural senses. Being a knower operates through our spirit.

It is the spirit of God quickening our faith to know by faith and not by sight; you know God, know his will and purpose, and know he is with you even though you cannot naturally trace him or feel him. This is a very important posture of maturity for the believer to attain because we are so emotion and sign driven. Though our flesh and emotions feel God, he is a spirit. We must know him by the spirit, engage him by the spirit, and be guided by our spirit. Emotions and signs can mislead us, but God's spirit is always pure and accurate. That is the reason David wanted a clean heart and a right spirit.

Psalms 51:10 Create in me a clean heart, O God; and renew a right spirit within me.

The psalmist knew God's spirit would guide him correctly. (Study *Romans 8* and ask God for revelation concerning hearing his voice over flesh and emotions).

Spiritual Senses- God speaks through our spiritual senses. When reading *Isaiah 6:1-8*, we find Isaiah experiencing a vision where all his senses were enthralled.

You may or may not literally experience sensation through your natural senses but please understand that what is being spoken is release through your spirit - the senses of the Holy Spirit in you.

You discern through your senses in the following ways:

- Seeing - eyes
- Hearing - ears
- Smelling - nose
- Tasting - mouth
- Touching - feeling, impression, sensation, physical awareness
- Perceiving - sensing, having a conscious awareness, sensation or recognition of something

Learn more about discerning through spiritual senses by obtaining my book, *Discerning The Voice Of God.*

Spiritual Translation – God may translate you inside a person's life, ministry, business, or situation. He may translate you to a region, inside the walls of the enemy's camp, covens, high wicked places, or to wherever he wants you to gain intel. It is important to be obedient to what he tells you to do and to maneuver at his leading as sometimes you may not be hidden during these translations. You must be mission focused and ready to attack or leave as God leads. Operating at his leading keeps you safe and from being tracked back to your home where counterattacks can occur. There was a time where I did not understand my gift and my soul would be so sensitive that as I slept, I would automatically astral project into the spirit realm. The witches, warlocks and demons would see me and would automatically attack me because the divine light of God that was around me. They knew I was the enemy even though I was no threat because I did not even know how I was ending up in the spirit realm, much less know how to contend with them. Sometimes they would track me back to my home and further attack me. It would be a year before I would be delivered from unauthorized soul astral projection, while learning how to yield to the Holy Spirit leading me in translation via my spirit. At his leading, I learned the purpose of this gift and how to be guided by him to do the work of the Lord and keep myself safe.

Intercessory Prayer & Warfare – God may lead you to stand in the gap and intercede and war as a scout. Sometimes he may translate you into the life and sphere of the person you are praying for or into the region they are ministering in and have you deal with sin issues, strongholds, principalities and powers, or spiritual wickedness in high places. He may have you pray in bold faith as he reveals matters that need to be addressed. It is important as scouts to be detailed in your ability to intercede and war. They need more than your blessing, encouragement, and empowerment. They need more than your elation and good will to pray for them with mediocre and religious prayers that do not confront darkness and will not fully cover, hedge in and overthrow the attacks that the person and ministry you are praying for will endure. They need you to grab hold and capture the vision of the destiny and calling on their lives and enter into the realms of the spirit, assert your authority to annihilate darkness, and to pursue, overtake, and recover on their behalf.

SCOUTING WITH VISION

A Scout's Visionary Stance and Mandate

Scouts position for the vision, write the vision, and make it plain for other scouts and ambassadors of the Lord to run with it and establish it in the earth.

Habakkuk 2:1-2 The Amplified Bible [OH, I know, I have been rash to talk out plainly this way to God!] I will [in my thinking] stand upon my post of observation and station myself on the tower or fortress, and will watch to see what He will say within me and what answer I will make [as His mouthpiece] to the perplexities of my complaint against Him. And the Lord answered me and said, Write the vision and engrave it so plainly upon tablets that everyone who passes may [be able to] read [it easily and quickly] as he hastens by.

Isaiah 21:6 For thus the Lord says to me, "Go, station the lookout, let him report what he sees.

Matthew 6:22-23 New International Bible The eye is the lamp of the body. If your eyes are healthy, your whole body will be full of light. But if your eyes are unhealthy, your whole body will be full of darkness. If then the light within you is darkness, how great is that darkness!

Luke 11:34 Aberrant Study Bible Your eye is the lamp of your body. When your vision is clear, your whole body also is full of light. But when it is poor, your body is full of darkness.

Matthew 13:11 He answered and said unto them, Because it is given unto you to know the mysteries of the kingdom of heaven, but to them it is not given.

Luke 8:10 He replied, "The knowledge of the mysteries of the kingdom of God has been given to you, but to others I speak in parables, so that, 'Though seeing, they may not see; though hearing, they may not understand.'

1Corinthians 2:12 But God has revealed it to us by the Spirit. The Spirit searches all things, even the deep things of God.

2Corinthians 5:7 For we walk by faith, not by sight.

Colossians 1:27 to whom God has chosen to make known among the Gentiles the glorious riches of this mystery, which is Christ in you, the hope of glory.

Scout Vision

A scout seeks God for, has clarity of, is equipped in, and can release strategically the vision for:

- Their destiny, calling, and the mandate upon their lives.
- Their regions and spheres of influences.
- The ministries, businesses, organizations, and networks of their assignment.
- Their leaders, ministry partners, and team members concerning mantles, destiny, callings, and kingdom mandates.
- Their generational line, lineages, inheritances, and how they and their generations line impact every generation.

Faith-filled Peering Scout

Scouts peer out into the deep. They have faith for the deeper matters and realms of God.

Psalms 42:7 Deep calleth unto deep at the noise of thy waterspouts: all thy waves and thy billows are gone over me.

Isaiah 62:6 On your walls, O Jerusalem, I have appointed watchmen; All day and all night they will never keep silent You who remind the LORD, take no rest for yourselves;

Luke 5:4 Now when he had left speaking, he said unto Simon, Launch out into the deep, and let down your nets for a draught.

John 21:6 He told them, "Cast the net on the right side of the boat, and you will find some." So they cast it there, and they were unable to haul it in because of the great number of fish.

Luke 5:5 "Master," Simon replied, "we have worked through the night without catching anything. But because You say so, I will let down the nets."

2Corinthians 4:17-18 For our light affliction, which is but for a moment, worketh for us a far more exceeding and eternal weight of glory; While we look not at the things which are seen, but at the things which are not seen: for the things which are seen are temporal; but the things which are not seen are eternal.

Hebrews 11:1 Now faith is the substance of things hoped for, the evidence of things not seen.

Hebrews 11:7 By faith Noah, when warned about things not yet seen, in godly fear built an ark to save his family. By faith he condemned the world and became heir of the righteousness that comes by faith.

Hebrews 11:27 By faith Moses left Egypt, not fearing the king's anger; he persevered because he saw Him who is invisible.

Scouts see minutes, days, months, years, seasons, ahead with clarity, and have the spiritual capacity to download the future - the horizon - into others.

Scouts do not wait for vision. Scouts peer into the unseen - into the dark - into the unknown - and bring the unseen into the seer realm. Scouts pursue God, his revelation, his knowledge, his counsel, his understanding, his wisdom, his might, his reverential fear, his mysteries, so they can have continual vision.

Scouts are not afraid of the dark - evil - demons - the devil - witches - witchcraft - the ungodly - the unrighteous - those in positions of authority - violent communities and territories - to confront - to judge - war - to fight - to be violent - to assert vengeance - to take the kingdom violently by force (*Study Psalms 91*). They know they are change agents and possess the armor to withstand and overthrow the wiles of the enemy.

Note: the previous paragraph is also an admonition for scouts to have excellent leadership who can guide and mentor their calling. Otherwise, a scout can become reckless and cause incredible damage, no matter how positive their intentions might have been. This is NOT a calling that can be released without maturity. The relationship between the scout and their spiritual leader must have transparency such that the scout can admit struggles and temptations. Trust the one(s) that God has placed to help you develop in your destiny.

Matthew 11:12 And from the days of John the Baptist until now the kingdom of heaven suffers violence, and the violent take it by force.

Scouts have night vision and honor night watches.

Psalm 119:148 My eyes stay open through the watches of the night, that I may meditate on [God's] promises.

SPIRITS THAT ATTACK MINISTERS

There are times I am ministering and am being attacked to the point where I will stop and pray out loud against the spirit that is attacking me. In other situations, I will call on my armorbearer to pray. My overseer sometimes has her armorbearer walking back and forth behind her interceding as she preaches to help fortify her from attacks.

Many ministers may have experienced these spirits but may not know what they were. That is because many of us expect and accept warfare as we preach or **some of us believe these experiences are our own inadequacies or mishaps rather than demonic interference at work.** I aim to expose these demons so they can be thwarted in the life of ministers. I decree that as you study this list, God will enable you to scout the spirit realm further such that you identify, expose, and cast out these demons that attack ministers.

Zapping Spirit - strikes or jolts, revelations and downloads that the minister received from God. One minute they have the information and the next minute it is gone; its suddenly depleted.

Blocking Spirit - Places a barrier in the spirit realm between the minister and God to block them from receiving fresh revelation and downloads as they minister. Spirit operate like an erected wall upon the brain, skull, imagination, or in the spirit realm to hinder and stifle revelation and communication between the minister and God.

Mind-Binding Spirit - Binds the mind to prevent the minister's brain from regurgitating and releasing the information where it can be understood. May cause confusion, cloudiness, disconcertedness. Sits upon the head and wraps around the around the head and presses then into the forehead, sides of the head, back of the head and sometimes the neck. Can also sit upon, wrap around, and press into the brain.

Mind-Blinding Spirit - Spirit blinds - covers - the spiritual and physical eyes, understanding, temples, and imagination of the minister to prevent them from seeing the revelation, seeing the vision, seeing what God is saying. The minister may experience blurred vision or literally blinding. They may trouble reading their notes, their bible, or the screen as they minister. This is sometimes the reason ministers use readers.

A minister's own anxiety, stress and pressure they have put upon themselves can bewitch them and causes the mind binding and mind blinding spirit to operate and attack them. Those who battle a spirit of perfectionism may experience this as perfectionism causes one to operate in their own strength rather than the strength and excellence of the Lord.

Mind-Controlling Spirit - Minister feels as if they are being controlled, manipulated, discombobulated, or maneuvered; may feel mental pain, pressure, a pressing down upon and around the head, or experience a headache. This spirit may operate like an octopus or squid having tentacles that may press around the head, eyes, ears, temples, neck and shoulders of the minister. They may have a difficult time focusing, remaining on or finishing a thought or subject; they may even babble or stutter.

Telepathy - Minister may feel as if they are receiving signals, impressions or pressured from an unseen force.

Perversion & Lust - The minister may experience perverted and lustful thoughts, images, and feelings, before, during or after ministry. This can be a demonic attack, witchcraft attack or they can be picking up on the sins of the people, ministry, or region; or the minister has a common sin issue as those he or she is ministering too. Some ministers may become explicit or carnal as they preach, especially if the have a sin issue; they are drawn into making comments that reflect what they are experiencing. Some ministers may be so appalled by what they are experiencing, they may have a difficult time ministering or they may minister a very strong rebuking word.

Twisted Thinking & Error - These spirits cause ministers to twist ideology, misquote God and scripture, use scriptures and concepts out of context; minister is more focused on building their case, and sounding good than being biblically grounded.

Spirit of Pride - The minister may yield to haughtiness and self-righteousness, minister more about self without relevance than about God; minister with a high self-importance that comes across as vain, boasting about self rather than glorifying God. Often you can tell this is an attack when it is not the normal character or nature of the minister.

Spirit of Heaviness, Sullenness & Depression - The minister may feel oppressed or depressed with a ungodly weightiness, sadness, may desire to cry for not reason, may baffled with different emotions, or sense of grief. May feel bogged down and like something is sitting on them. May have a difficult time praising, worshipping and exalting Jesus.

Spirit of Fear, Panic, & Anxiety - You probably have watched a preacher experience these spirits and not even know it. You thought they were rambling, sweating, turning red, pulling on their tie, unbuttoning and taking off clothes, was them being hot from that fiery preaching. Sometimes this is the case and other times a preacher may be battling these spirits. They may display uncontrollable profusion, shaking or panic. They may have moments where they are starring off in space or at their notes while trying to gather themselves. Some ministers may experience internal anxiety, apprehension, panic around the heart, rapid heartbeat, thought racing, nausea, or urge to go to the restroom.

Spirit of Mockery & Insecurity - This spirit taunts the minister before, during, and after they are preaching. It makes them feel inadequate, like the people are laughing at them or not listening to them, like what they are ministering is insignificant. It will have them questioning God and themselves. The minister will hear this spirit literally laughing, throwing shade, belittling them. Sometimes the minister will see this spirit working through people in the audience. They will see this sport use people to laugh at them, taunting them, making fun of them as they minister.

Spirit of Religion and Tradition - These spirits operate through suffocation to snuff out the Holy Spirit, glory and presence of God from operating upon and through the minister. The minister may feel a literal strangulation or suffocation, may feel like his or her throat or respiratory system is shutting down, may start coughing, gagging, having trouble breathing. Religion will erect like a fog, dark blanket type cloud or wall and clog up the heavenlies over a service. It will weigh down heavy on the people, separate them from the preacher and the preached word, and cause them to become mute or death and dumb. They will stop agreeing with the word as they go into a stupor type state. It will close the people off from experiencing the full effect of God's plan through that word. It will be as if they are a movie as they are disconnected from what is being released. They may also appear in awe of some of the revelation and signs that manifest through the minister, but nothing will be planted in their spirits as they are disconnected. The ministry will not manifest change or transformation in the lives of the people, the church and/or the atmosphere because there is a barrier between them and what is going forth.

Tradition will feel like barricade of resistance which usually presents itself as control, judgment, or refusal to receive. Tradition can be unassuming at first as it tends to be an invisible erected barrier, but the minister will feel it coming to the forefront the minute it challenges a tradition within the people, ministry, or region. Often tradition hits back by trying to bind, shutdown, or suffocate the minister physically and spiritually. It will also release energies of intimidation and control to coward the minister to back off the subject where its high places can remain in tack.

Witchcraft - Hexes, vexes, spells, hoodoo, voodoo, charms, bewitching slander, etc., sent to influence, bind, distract, or stifle the minister in effectively preaching the word of God.

Fiery Darts - Inflamed angry, grievous, lustful, venomous word curses coming from demons, witches, warlocks, wicked people, and ignorant people. May will physically feel like a demonic angry fire or burning sensation. (Quench these word curses)

Friendly Fire - Darts coming from past and present friends and acquaintances who are speaking - releasing ill words against the minister.

Sickness - Afflictions and infirmities sent to bind and distract the minister with physical ailments. Headaches, stomach aches, nausea, respiratory and sinus issues, heart issues, blood pressure issues, pains in the back, neck, feet, knees, temple, hips, are common attacks ministers experience when preaching the gospel. Some of this is due to witchcraft being sent to afflict certain areas. Demons are also sent to oppress these areas.

Tracking Spirits – These are demonic agents who are assigned to gather intel on a minister and then report it back to their demonic camp. They track minister by their smell, footprints, voice, fliers, and any other means. They will track the minister from place to place as they move about everyday life, through computer systems and other computerized intel, etc. They will even track you to church and ministry events. They lurk around–ease dropping on prayers and conversations, to acquire information about the minister then report back so that demonic assignments can be released against them. Sometimes these spirits can be sensed or felt while they follow a person. You know those times it feels like something is following you. It is probably a tracker. They tend to live on the airways, so they rarely will use a body. Although they will oppress people in the minister's inner circle and track them that way. Or they will follow people in minister's inner circle and track them. Psychics, high priests work with these spirits to track clients and gather intel, so they can have information to share when the person comes for their session. It appears as if the psychic possesses information that only someone in one's private life could have known. They do because the demon tracked the person.

Watcher Spirits - Are spirits that are sent to spy on you after the tracker spirit has shared information on you with his demonic camp. Watchers report on your progress so that further demonic assignments can be released against you. Watcher spirits will even travel to different places as you travel or send messages to other regions that you are coming, share the intel regarding you, so that the demons in that region can be aware of what you will be doing, and can find a way to counterattack your productivity and progress. Especially if you are trying to save souls for Jesus. In the past, I use to see these spirits traveling by the airplane when I am going out of town to do ministry. I have learned to pray to cancel their assignments, so they do not track me. Many people share all kinds of personal information on your social media pages. Watcher spirits are sharing that information with the demonic camp. The enemy knew where and how to attack the person at because it is on their Facebook page. In the spirit realm, the devil has a demonic library where he keeps files, especially of people who have great callings on their lives. I have seen these libraries and some of these files. Also, the systems of this world, ignorantly help these spirits to collect and maintain information on us. We are constantly being asked for our updated email address, cellphone numbers, etc., when we go in stores or when conducting business transactions.

Scanner Spirits – Use electronics like computers, phones, cameras, to track and gain intel on a minister. They operate as spies that travel throughout areas and regions and transport information to different demonic camps and demonic rankings. They inspect, observe, survey their enemy or a territory for exploitation and military purposes.

Eavesdropping Spirits – Similar to watcher spirits, these demons lurk around ease dropping on the minister's life, conversations, loved ones and friends, to gain intel that can be used for demonic attack. Often these spirits will acquire personal information and then use it to infiltrate a minister's life to gain further personal insight and even to stage a personal attack. It is nothing like being attacked by someone close to a person. Eavesdropping spirits are good for gaining the heart and favor of a minister through personal intel, then causing drama, betrayal, and heartbreak.

Demonic Agents – Are gang or police type spirits that are sent to intimidate, attack, or seize a minister where they fear or are unable to minister. These spirits love to attack through the dream realm or at night. Sometimes they have on black clothing or maybe dressed similar like a gang or officers. They tend to surround or corner the person in a dream or within the spirit realm then attack. Sometimes these spirits operate at crosswords on highways or roads. They may operate through police officers or those superior in ministry, community, or business in effort to intimidate, control, or seize a minister. They like to back ministers in a corner where they will make decisions that usually are outside of the perfect will of God.

DISCERNING DEMONIC LASHINGS

The enemy will strive to lay siege against a ministry or person in by causing front lash, backlash, side lash, lash from hell to make ministry difficult. The military concept of laying siege includes cutting off supply lines, especially water and allies. In ancient times, it included catapulting dead animals into a city to cause disease epidemics.

LASH

From experience, I define lash as a *"sudden, swift, forceful, strong, or violent attack via words or actions to cause distraction, backward movement, draw back, shrink back, alarm, fear, dread, pain, and punishment regarding operating in ministry, destiny, or one's life vision."*

This quote is from Apostle Jackie Green's *Church Planters Spiritual Warfare Manual, "Lashes are blockages, hindrances and curses sent to the believer who is about to do great damage to the Kingdom of Darkness. The enemy tries to stop the Kingdom Work before it begins. It is a sign that the Kingdom of God already has the victory and fear is struck in the heart of demons."*

FRONT LASH

This specific lashing will manifest before a ministry event, major SHIFT, or significant life event. It surfaces to delay, stifle, and thwart the person, ministry, event, vision. It comes through friends, family, acquaintances, covenants, strangers, witches, warlocks, saints, situations, the weather, the atmosphere, or spiritual wickedness in high places. It can come through one person or a group. It may appear in one situation or many situations; therefore, you cannot afford to think that one victory in one battle wins the whole war. It can manifest as demonic or unhealthy emotional activity, conflict, or competition. It manifests when a believer is vulnerable even during spiritual vulnerability for it does not have to be a sin or emotional issue. It comes through those that gain intel on a person or event then are used to attack it so that it will not be penetrating, transforming, successful, or establishing. It comes when God has identified, aligned, processed, and established you in a significant SHIFT that you are about to embark upon, with fresh visions and assignments, or with a major ministry and destiny assignments.

Apostle Jackie Green's Front Lash Manifestations:
- Unexpected storms and circumstances.
- Demonic surprises.
- Sudden illness.
- Bombarded distractions.
- Overwhelmed and burdened.
- If you are fasting, fatigue, fretful, heavy sleep, irritable.
- Time waster spirits and the Spoiler is sent to take your joy before the event.
- Remember we are not fighting one another, but against principalities and powers so be mindful of petty arguments and squabbles among those in the team, in marriages and families, on the job, etc.
- Attacks on the job just before the conference or event.
- MAGNIFICATION of family and financial issues.
- Things breaking down and malfunctioning to release FRUSTRATION
- DELAYS, TRAFFIC JAMS, FLIGHT PROBLEMS, FOOD POISONING, LOSING THINGS.
- THE SPIRIT OF INVISIBLE – spirits that operate behind the scenes to attack a person, event, ministry, or vision.
- THE SPIRIT OF ACCIDENTS – crossroad spirits that operate on the road and airways to cause incidents, delays, and tragedy.
- Demonic spirits can hold people in a region where people are not able to travel to the conference.
- Attacks from family and spouse or those close to you.

- Indirect warfare–attacks on those close to you to drain and distract you.

1Peter 5:8 Be sober-minded and alert. Your adversary the devil prowls around like a roaring lion, seeking someone to devour.

John10:10 The thief cometh not, but for to steal, and to kill, and to destroy: I am come that they might have life, and that they might have it more abundantly.

Job 1:7, 2:2 And the LORD said unto Satan, From whence comest thou? And Satan answered the LORD, and said, from going to and fro in the earth, and from walking up and down in it.

SIDEBAR REVELATION: The devil was looking to kill, steal, and destroy, when he entered heaven and God inquired of his whereabouts.

Matthew 4:1 Then Jesus was led up by the Spirit into the wilderness to be tempted by the Devil

SIDEBAR REVELATION: The devil loves to get believers alone and thwart what is about to occur or is occurring in their lives – can be front lash or backlash.

Matthew 4:2,3 He fasted forty days and forty nights, and afterwards He was famished. The tempter came and said to Him, "If indeed You are the Son of God, command these stones to become loaves of bread."

SIDEBAR REVELATION: Jesus had just finished a fast and his flesh was vulnerable to wanting food and strength and here comes the devil – can be front lash or backlash.

Matthew 3:16,17;4:1 And when Jesus had been baptized, just as He came up from the water, suddenly the heavens were opened to Him and He saw the Spirit of God descending like a dove and alighting on Him. And a voice from heaven said, "This is My Son, the Beloved, with whom I am well pleased." Then Jesus was led by the Spirit into the desert to be tempted by the Devil

SIDEBAR REVELATION: As soon as God position, identifies, and aligns you, the devil comes for your seeds, fruit, process, and establishment. Jesus had not even begun walking in this impartation yet, and here the devil comes – can be front lash or backlash.

BACKLASH

Apostle Jackie Green's Definition of Backlash, *"All-out war against the saints from the Devil, retaliation and getting even with the saints of God for damages incurred by the Kingdom of darkness. It is a sign that the Kingdom of God has advanced. Believers that are doing Kingdom work especially casting out demons and healing the sick and pulling souls out of the kingdom of darkness must expect backlash."*

Manifestations of Spirits of Backlash: (cited from Win Worley's book, Battling the Hosts of Hell.)

- The pressures of the enemy are arranged to stop you from pursuing real spiritual warfare.
- Apparitions, physical pains, and sickness.
- Sound of footsteps.
- Black figures in the room or hovering over our bed.
- Ghostly hands touching.
- Voices whispering.
- Panting hot breath on the face.
- Waves of icy air moving across or around.

Taquetta's Backlash Revelation

Definition: Punishment and pain inflicted through words or actions due to operating in ministry, destiny, or one's life vision. Backlash manifests suddenly, swiftly, forcefully, or can even be subtle and then dreadful. The purpose of backlash is to make you wish you never did what God told you to do and to instill fear, drawback, shrinkage, delay, or dread in operating in present and future ministry and destiny endeavors.

> *The purpose of backlash is to make you wish you never did what God told you to do.*

Manifestations of Spirits of Backlash

Backlash is retaliation in the form of anger, resentment, kickback, counterattack that can generate as psychological or emotional warfare, sickness, trauma, hardship, accidents, or tragedy. Sometimes the lashing you released upon the enemy seems to now be hitting you and with an even stronger force. This can feel like a boomerang effect as if your annihilation of the enemy fired back at you. A boomerang is not actually occurring as your work accomplished what God required. The enemy is lashing back from what was done to his kingdom.

Backlash can also come through the contamination of work done in ministry, especially if a ministered moved without God's authority or moved out of their heart or flesh and not out of their spirit. It can also come in the form of rejection and persecution.

1Kings 18:19-46 Study how Elijah endured backlash from his showdown with Jezebel and the prophets of Baal.

1Timothy 5:22 Lay hands suddenly on no man, neither be a partaker of other men's sins: keep yourself pure. (This is an example of moving out of your heart, flesh, own authority).

Proverbs 19:19 The Message Bible Let angry people endure the backlash of their own anger; if you try to make it better, you'll only make it worse.

SIDEBAR REVELATION: Sometimes people can become challenged or in error by the ministry you release, consequentially using it against you.

Matthew 10:14 And whoever will not receive you, nor hear your words, when you leave that house or city, shake off the dust of your feet.

SIDEBAR REVELATION: Rejection will come for you in the form of backlash when doing the work of the gospel.

Matthew 5:10 Blessed are they which are persecuted for righteousness' sake: for theirs is the kingdom of heaven.

Mark 10:30 But he shall receive an hundredfold now in this time, houses, and brethren, and sisters, and mothers, and children, and lands, with persecutions; and in the world to come eternal life.

Luke 4:13 When the Devil had finished every test, he departed from Him until an opportune time.

LASH FROM HELL

Taquetta's Revelation Regarding Lashes From Hell

Lashing that comes with dark, demeaning, evil, death defying torture, igniting to waste time, pest, plague and destroy a person, situation, ministry, event, destiny, or vision.

Matthew 16:15-19 He saith unto them, But whom say ye that I am? And Simon Peter answered and said, Thou art the Christ, the Son of the living God. And Jesus answered and said unto him, Blessed art thou, Simon Barjona: for flesh and blood hath not revealed it unto thee, but my Father which is in heaven. And I say also unto

*thee, That thou art Peter, and upon this rock I will build my
church; and the gates of hell shall not prevail against it. And I will
give unto thee the keys of the kingdom of heaven: and whatsoever
thou shalt bind on earth shall be bound in heaven: and whatsoever
thou shalt loose on earth shall be loosed in heaven.*

*Psalms 91:3 Surely he shall deliver thee from the snare of the
fowler (the baitlayer), and from the noisome pestilence.*

Noisome is *hawwâ* in Hebrew:
- in the sense of eagerly coveting and rushing upon;
- by implication, of falling); desire;
- also ruin: — calamity, iniquity, mischief, mischievous
  (thing), naughtiness, naughty, noisome, perverse thing,
  substance, very wickedness, engulfing ruin, destruction,
  calamity.

*Psalms 91:5-6 The Amplified Bible You shall not be afraid of the
terror of the night, nor of the arrow (the evil plots and slanders of
the wicked) that flies by day, Nor of the pestilence (destroying
plagues and disease) that stalks in darkness, nor of the destruction
and sudden death that surprise and lay waste at noonday.*

*Psalms 22:16-22 For [like a pack of] dogs they have encompassed
me; a company of evildoers has encircled me, they pierced my
hands and my feet. I can count all my bones; [the evildoers] gaze
at me. They part my clothing among them and cast lots for my
raiment (a long, shirt like garment, a seamless under tunic).) But
be not far from me, O Lord; O my Help, hasten to aid me! Deliver
my life from the sword, my dear life [my only one] from the power
of the dog [the agent of execution]. Save me from the lion's mouth;
for You have answered me [kindly] from the horns of the wild
oxen. I will declare Your name to my brethren; in the midst of the
congregation will I praise You.*

*Psalms 59:5-7 You, O Lord God of hosts, the God of Israel, arise
to visit all the nations; spare none and be not merciful to any who
treacherously plot evil. Selah [pause, and calmly think of that]!*

They return at evening, they howl and snarl like dogs, and go [prowling] about the city. Behold, they belch out [insults] with their mouths; swords [of sarcasm, ridicule, slander, and lies] are in their lips, for who, they think, hears us? (also study verse 1-14)

Psalms 18:5 The cords of Sheol surrounded me; The snares of death confronted me.

Psalms 107:20 He sent His word and healed them, And delivered them from their destructions.

Proverbs 1:12 Let us swallow them alive like Sheol, Even whole, as those who go down to the pit;

Proverbs 30:16 Sheol, and the barren womb, Earth that is never satisfied with water, And fire that never says, "Enough."

Jonah 2:2 And he said, "I called out of my distress to the LORD, And He answered me I cried for help from the depth of Sheol; You heard my voice.

Psalms 88:11-12 Will Your lovingkindness be declared in the grave, Your faithfulness in Abaddon? Will Your wonders be made known in the darkness? And Your righteousness in the land of forgetfulness?

Psalms 16:10 For You will not abandon my soul to Sheol; Nor will You allow Your Holy One to undergo decay.

Psalms 30:3 O LORD, You have brought up my soul from Sheol; You have kept me alive, that I would not go down to the pit.

Psalms 49:15 But God will redeem my soul from the power of Sheol, For He will receive me. Selah.

Psalms 86:13 For Your lovingkindness toward me is great, And You have delivered my soul from the depths of Sheol.

Manifestations of Spirits of Hell

- Dark, evil, and does not feel from this world.
- Causes distress, anguish, misery and torment that feels like punishment even though you are not guilty or do not have any open doors or unrepentant or unprocessed sin.
- Affliction or experience that feels terminal, contagious, plagued, diseased, without any cure or hope.
- Evil plots accompanied by extreme disorder or confusion.
- Appears as if you are inside of a coffin, grave, or as if death is all around you.
- Can feel like you are at rock bottom, in a bottom pit, not just hopeless but literally pulled down to a low place, low pit, low grave, and cannot get out.
- The soul can feel like it is in hell even though you are alive and living in the earth realm.
- May feel an increased darkness and eeriness at night and even during the day.
- May incur demonic visitations from the hounds of hell, agents of hell, high ranking witches and warlocks, in effort to release curses, death, intimidation, control, and bewitching manipulation.

SIDE LASH

Taquetta's Side Lash Revelation

Definition: Deceitful, scornful, disparaging, or amorous acts and glances from the enemy that is indirect or evasive. It may come through an indirect situation or person and hit you. It may come subtly, without warning, through a situation that appears innocent or harmless, or through a situation that you have warning about but have your guard down; or you may perceive yourself to be equipped to handle the situation or to be in a place in God where you would not possibly succumb to that type of behavior. It can also come due to associate and relationship where it is not about you but you are hit because you know a person, are in relationship with a person, or you have insight or contact with that particularly situation. The enemy cannot get directly to you so he will use people close to you or who have access to you to hit you. Sometimes there will be open doors due to issues that are already in the relationship and the enemy will use that to gain entrance to you. Sometimes situations will manifest seemingly out of nowhere where the person becomes an open door to lash you.

Often you are already aware of the person's issues and know this is a lash. Sometimes the manifestation is uncharacteristic of the individual's personality, so you know it is a lash. Sometimes the enemy can gain a foothold and there is no obvious indication of the reason the person or situation became a door for the lash.

Manifestations of Spirits of Side Lash

- Can hit like a side swipe, broadsided, slippery slope, or fiery dart.
- Can hit when you are turning a corner or SHIFT around a curve in your life, ministry, or vision.
- Can catch you off guard because it is often unexpected. It can hit when your guard is down because it is coming through something or someone. It is the result of tracking direct movement and comes in laterally.
- Can cause you to stumble or throw you off because of the way it comes in. It is a diversionary tactic.
- Can sometimes operates illegally as sometimes it is not even your issues or situation to bear but tries to draw you in by association with someone or something. Being a fixer, rescuer, living through wells of obligation, need for validation, need to feel loved, can cause a person to be drawn into side lash because they are not discerning of how the enemy operates or they discern too late. They are already in the midst trying to fix or get a need met before they realize that have been hit and they are carrying a burden that has nothing to do with God or the current ministry or life situation at hand. It is important to know the posture God desires you to have in each season, ministry engagement, as you operate in destiny and your life's vision so you can quickly discern side lash and not leave your postured position to engage in side lash.

2Corinthians 2:11 If you forgive anyone, I also forgive him. And if I have forgiven anything, I have forgiven it in the presence of Christ for your sake, 11in order that Satan should not outwit us. For we are not unaware of his schemes.

Matthew 16:22-23 And Peter took Him aside and began to rebuke Him, saying, "God forbid it, Lord! This must never happen to You." But He turned and said to Peter, "Get behind Me, Satan!

You are a stumbling block to Me; for you are setting your mind not on divine things but on human things."

Luke 22:31 Simon, Simon, Satan has asked to sift each of you like wheat.

SIDEBAR REVELATION: Simon did not think the enemy could hit him. He had his guard down in thinking he was somewhere in God that he was not and was hit through the warfare of Jesus fulfilling his destiny of dying on the cross. He was even warned but still did not discern the side lash until he had already fell prey and sinned against Jesus.

1Peter 5:8 Be sober-minded and alert. Your adversary the devil prowls around like a roaring lion, seeking someone to devour.

2Corinthians 11:3,14 But I fear, lest by any means, as the serpent beguiled Eve through his subtilty, so your minds should be corrupted from the simplicity that is in Christ.

1Chronicles 21:1,2 And Satan stood up against Israel, and provoked David to number Israel.

Mark 4:15 Some are like the seeds along the path, where the word is sown. As soon as they hear it, Satan comes and takes away the word that was sown in them.

PETTY LASH

Taquetta's Petty Lash Revelation

Definition: Trivial, unimportant, insignificant, small conflicts meant to distract, punish and weary a person from focusing on important matters. Petty lash will lack substance or value and will appear bigger than it really is. You will feel oppressed and punished for something that is more of a pet peeve or passive aggressive motive than a validated issue. It is essential not to yield to the distractions and frustrations of petty lash as this is what gives it embedded power over you. Recognizing and calling it for what it is and separating yourself from relinquishes its oppression while keeping you under the protection of God is the most effective response to this attack.

THWARTING LASHINGS

Know that the enemy will come with lashing. You are in a war so you must be violent, conscious, and expect that the enemy will come for you. He will not win but he will come. It is his job to come. He roams in expectation to attack and devour. Pray to thwart the attacks of front lash, backlash, side lash, and lash from hell by being discerning and offensive and canceling their assignments before they come for you. Assert your authority so that even if lashes come, they have no effect on you. Be led by your spirit not by your heart and flesh so you will not be drawn into unnecessary warfare and lashings.

Matthew 11:12 And from the days of John the Baptist until now the kingdom of heaven suffereth violence, and the violent take it by force.

Ephesians 6:12-13 For we wrestle not against flesh and blood, but against principalities, against powers, against the rulers of the darkness of this world, against spiritual wickedness in high places. Wherefore take unto you the whole armour of God, that ye may be able to withstand in the evil day, and having done all, to stand.

Luke 10:19 Behold, I give unto you power to tread on serpents and scorpions, and over all the power of the enemy: and nothing shall by any means hurt you.

Mark 16:18 They shall take up serpents; and if they drink any deadly thing, it shall not hurt them; they shall lay hands on the sick, and they shall recover.

Isaiah 59:19 So shall they fear the name of the Lord from the west, and his glory from the rising of the sun. When the enemy shall come in like a flood, the Spirit of the Lord shall lift up a standard against him.

2Timothy 4:18 The Lord will rescue me from every evil attack and save me for His heavenly kingdom. To Him be the glory forever and ever. Amen.

DEMON COLLABORATION AMONG REGIONS: CONFEDERACY

From time to time, when scouting in spiritual warfare or visiting different regions, I see principalities and powers collaborating to attack a ministry or minister. This can also be called demonic confederacy. A demonic confederacy is when principalities and powers, evil workers, and other forces of darkness make alliances with one another to come into agreement to attack and siege a person, place, situation, region or nation. These demons share information They are sharing across regions and nations to release continual assaults against saints, ministers, and ministries. They collaborate with watcher spirits, squatter spirits, scanner spirits, and demonic agents collecting intel and then using it to attack, while also sharing this information to keep the attack going within and among regions. They are creating sieges so those or that which they are attacking are closed in on every side and cannot stop the continuous warfare that is being released against them.

There are also instances where the principalities and powers have been able to shut down in one region, therefore there is a summons and agreement with principalities and powers from other regions to come and attack on their behalf. A secondary strategy is that they will call for reinforcements from other regions to strengthen their battle against a ministry or minister. As a scout, I have also witnessed demons from other regions track and spy on ministers and ministries then release intel to regions they reside in or are in their itinerary.

One day I received this message from one of my mentees who was attending a revival conference I was having at my center.

When I woke up, I looked at the blinds. The sunlight was jumping horizontally as the light was shining vertically. I closed my eyes and looked again, and the same thing was happening. There's a principality that has been sent and is walking about like a

Godzilla. I can hear the footsteps as he is walking about. This principality is foreign to this region. It has been summoned.

Many ministers would have thought this information was weird and perhaps even ignored it. Demons know the power of unity and collaboration. Let's examine the story of Daniel where he went on a fast, seeking an answer to prayer. He was visited by an angel who told him his prayer was answered on the first day, but a principality had been contending against his answered prayers for 21 days. The angel encouraged Daniel and gave him revelation. He then said he was returning to fight the prince of Persia but told Daniel that as he went, a principality from Greece would come to contend against him. WHAT????? Let me give you some time to read it before I/we SHIFT onward.

Daniel 10:12-21 And [the angel] said to me, O Daniel, you greatly beloved man, understand the words that I speak to you and stand upright, for to you I am now sent. And while he was saying this word to me, I stood up trembling. Then he said to me, Fear not, Daniel, for from the first day that you set your mind and heart to understand and to humble yourself before your God, your words were heard, and I have come as a consequence of [and in response to] your words.

But the prince of the kingdom of Persia withstood me for twenty-one days. Then Michael, one of the chief [of the celestial] princes, came to help me, for I remained there with the kings of Persia. Now I have come to make you understand what is to befall your people in the latter days, for the vision is for [many] days yet to come. When he had spoken to me according to these words, I turned my face toward the ground and was dumb. And behold, one in the likeness of the sons of men touched my lips. Then I opened my mouth and spoke. I said to him who stood before me, O my lord, by reason of the vision sorrows and pains have come upon me, and I retain no strength. For how can my lord's servant [who is so feeble] talk with this my lord? For now no strength remains in me, nor is there any breath left in me.

Then there touched me again one whose appearance was like that of a man, and he strengthened me. And he said, O man greatly beloved, fear not! Peace be to you! Be strong, yes, be strong. And when he had spoken to me, I was strengthened and said, Let my lord speak, for you have strengthened me. Then he said, Do you know why I have come to you? And now I will return to fight with the [hostile] prince of Persia; and when I have gone, behold, the [hostile] prince of Greece will come. But I will tell you what is inscribed in the writing of truth or the Book of Truth. There is no one who holds with me and strengthens himself against these [hostile spirit forces] except Michael, your prince [national guardian angel].

Persia was an idolatrous region. Daniel was already known for his excellent spirit, dream interpretation, favor with the king and the people, unwillingness to bow to other gods, and freedom to serve his God - the only true and loving God - despite living in this idolatrous region where his people were slaves. Satan did not want Daniel to have understanding of future events, so he warred against him receiving answers and revelation to his prayers. Satan even sent a principality from Greece to further oppose Daniel.

Those that carry detailed prophetic revelation will be resisted by principalities and powers, especially if it saves and transforms lives, significantly reform regions and generations and establish and advance the kingdom of God. The angel Michael made Daniel aware of this attack and gave him truth regarding him overcoming it. Often ministers and ministries are not cognizant of demonic contention; therefore, they lack strategy to combat them. This leaves them (and their followers) vulnerable and exposed to attack. A few great keys we can learn from Daniel is during this time of great download, he postured himself in consecration and fasting which positioned him inside the secret place of the Lord. This released the Archangel Michael to work on his behalf and to reveal insight about further attacks. There are some seasons where ministers and ministries must be discerning about SHIFTING deeper into the secret place of the Lord. We must know when to retreat so that we can gain intel on the enemy and how he is opposing what God has granted to our hands. We must also know that the enemy wants to oppose what is in us and that his kingdom will band together against us. We can no longer be ignorant regarding the enemy's warfare tactics.

For ministers and ministries ministering in different regions, especially if you have a constant ministry itinerary, are planting works in various territories, have been called to govern different territories, it is important to shutdown collaborating operations of demons within and across regions. You may be experiencing warfare because you have annihilated it in your region, but it is coming from another region. While you are collaborating for God, the demonic confederacy is collaborating for Satan's kingdom.

Praying Against Collaborating Operations:

1. Learn the principalities and powers in the region of your assignment, so you can discern what demonic spirits may come against you, as often demons attack as it relates to our purpose and calling.
2. Decree that you and your ministry operate as a stealth bomber so you can go in and out of regions undetected. *Psalms 18:28-29* references the stealth bomber anointing. *For thou wilt light my candle: the Lord my God will enlighten my darkness. For by thee I have run through a troop; and by my God have I leaped over a wall.*
3. Close any gateways and landlines in the spirit to which demons can track you and as you go in and out of regions.
4. Declare any intel about you (media and any of the five senses), cannot be tracked by principalities, demonic agents, scanner spirits, watcher spirits, witches, warlocks, or any other force assigned to you by the kingdom of darkness.
5. Nullify the powers of any assignments being collaborated about you by demonic spirits, witches, warlocks, wicked and ignorant people.

6. Draw a blood, fire and glory line around regions you are in and declare that no demon from other regions can cross the threshold.

SIEGE WARFARE

Scouts can be used as skilled soldiers that form sieges to annihilate devils, demonic camps, and wickedness.

Siege in Latin means *"to sit."*

Siege is *"masar"* in *Hebrew*
- *besieged, bulwark, defense, fenced,*
- *fortress strong (hold), tower, enclosure, entrenchment.*

Siege warfare is a military operation in which blockades are set up to surround a town or building, a city or fortress, cutting off essential supplies, with the aim of compelling the surrender of those inside.   A siege can be against a person, group of people, troops of a military group, demons, demon camps, witchcraft covens, ungodly high places, etc. A siege can be a spiritual formation around situations and events for the purposes of causing a surrender to the purposes and judgements of God.

Spiritual provision is blocked causing hopelessness, helplessness, detriment, ultimatums, starvation, thirst, or disease. The person, place, thing, or matter being sieged is reduced to consuming and using all their supply, while resorting to eating and drinking whatever is available as a means of survival. In some historical siege situations, the enemy has been reduced to eating family pets, animals that are generally used for labor rather than consumption, household items and materials, and even each other (cannibalism).

The goal of siege warfare is to corner or surround an enemy so that they have no way of escaping to obtain their needs, and thus are forced to surrender or trapped where their lives can become captive and/or destroyed. Siege warfare requires specific strategizing and positioning. We discern this in Ezekiel when God uses Ezekiel to lay a siege against the rebellion of Jerusalem.

Ezekiel 2:3-4 And lay siege against it, and build a fort against it, and cast a mount against it; set the camp also against it, and set battering rams against it round about. Moreover take thou unto thee an iron pan, and set it for a wall of iron between thee and the city: and set thy face against it, and it shall be besieged, and thou shalt lay siege against it. This shall be a sign to the house of Israel.

Ezekiel was to represent:

- Years of Jerusalem's established idolatry.
- The current judging destruction of the city due to their provoking sins.
- The judgement that was to come if they did not repent and return in right relationship and salvation with God.
- Ezekiel was constantly activating and releasing the following siege against the people and the region.
- Building – spiritually and or naturally creating sidewalls or towers of fortification.
- Mounting – spiritually and or naturally creating a military mound or bank to launch an attack from a raised position.
- Setting battering rams – spiritually and naturally encamping round about and continuously hitting with the words, weaponry of God from every side.
- Laying siege – laying wait in the establishment of the siege to clearly assert that there was sieging and judgment occurring, while provoking a surrendering and turning before the ultimate judgement death was released.
- Setting an iron pan for a wall – spiritually and naturally demonstrating that this was a strong, hard, solid word, stance and armor of judgement that needed to be taken seriously.
- Set in face – spiritually and naturally facing the people and the region head on, while confronting and enduring the weight, challenges, lashings, and stance of the siege.

- Besiege – spiritually and naturally further hemming in, fastening in, fencing in, entrenching that which is being sieged to bring them to distress and subjectivity.
- Being a sign – spiritually and naturally becoming the prophetic banner, model, and representation of the word, judgement, and justice that is being sought through the siege.

As we read the life of Ezekiel, we know that siege warfare can be hard work and requires sacrifice. A siege is not a negotiation, so those or that which is being sieged may not willingly or quickly surrender. In a negotiation, mutual discussions and arrangements of terms and agreements are made to get the person, place, or thing to conform or surrender. Ultimately, the goal of a siege is to deplete the opposition until those under siege submit and surrender to the fate being thrust upon them. This requires sitting fully in sovereign authority, while building, mounting, battering, and laying wait in a scout position of intercession and warfare until that which is sieged surrenders, or is so sieged that you can close in and annihilate them.

Godly Scouts Sieging the Enemy as a Team

While in a prayer meeting, assign scouts where they are position in authority surrounding the enemy – north, south, east, west, above, and beneath – while trapping them inside your fortification. As a prophetic act, each scout can go to this direction in the room. As you all seize the enemy and his camp, seek God for a prayer strategy and use it to demand or provoke their surrender; You can also have each scout pray or praise and worship, while engaging in this prophetic act to ambush and annihilate the enemy. Another outcome is that the opposition turn on themselves and become their own murderous destruction (Study 2Chronicles 20).

Sieging from Within and Without

In *Deuteronomy 20*, God provides Joshua strategy for how to conquer the land of their enemies, particularly the Hittites, and the Amorites, the Canaanites, and the Perizzites.

Deuteronomy 20:10-14 When you draw near to a city to fight against it, offer terms of peace to it. And if its answer to you is peace and it opens to you, then all the people who are found in it shall do forced labor for you and shall serve you. But if it makes no peace with you, but makes war against you, then you shall besiege it; and when The Lord your God gives it into your hand you shall put all its males to the sword, but the women and the little ones, the cattle, and everything else in the city, all its spoil, you shall take as booty for yourselves; and you shall enjoy the spoil of your enemies, which The Lord your God has given you.

In *Joshua 5-6*, God gives Joshua and Israel a prophetic siege against Jericho. They had sieged the region until none could enter or leave. They were subject to Joshua and his army and were encircled by their authority. This siege was interesting because Jericho was a walled city. Because Joshua and company followed the strategy of the Lord, they were able to collapse the wall and takeover the land of Jericho.

Joshua 6:1-2 Now Jericho was shut up from within and from without because of the people of Israel; none went out, and none came in. And The Lord said to Joshua, "See, I have given into your hand Jericho, with its king and mighty men of valor."

Both sieges were essential to the Israelites entering the promise land. When God has released promises and prophecies regarding blessings, favor, wealth, overtaking territory, and kingdom advancement, a spiritual siege may be necessary to overthrow the inhabitants and evacuate them from the property. It is imperative to be obedient regarding how to administer the siege. Especially since what we may consider spoils of war, God may deem sinful, unlawful, ungodly, not fit for godly sacrifice or use, and therefore, need to be destroyed. By our own opinion or thought, we may mistakenly believe this territory to be the promised land and inhabit there, when it may only be a pathway to the promise land. Only God can provide this insight. Seek him for strategy as it will ensure that his desires, purposes, promises, and prophecies manifests appropriate through the siege.

Demonic Sieges

Scouts need to know that siege warfare can be used by the demonic realm against us as saints of God.

Demons Sieging on Every Side

The enemy will attempt to set sieges against saints by forming demonic alliances, hedging the person's life, health, and affairs inside a demonic portal, while attacking from every side. The goal is to so weary or deplete the person until they no longer want to serve God, walk in their destiny and calling, do ministry, or are so weary that they are unproductive, or cannot follow through with the work of the Lord. One of the keys to a successful siege is to psychologically manipulate those inside the siege until they believe no help is coming. When we start feeling that God cannot be our help, we have entered a critical state of collapse.

Witchcraft Siege

Witches and warlocks use what is called cage spirits or cage incantations to siege people and saints.   A cage is a boxlike enclosure having wires, bars, nets, snares, basket, stick or stone outline spell boxes, ley lines, or the like, for confining, demonically displaying, imprisoning, and trapping a person, place, or thing. By using spells and demons, saints are placed in spiritual cage where they are confined and are sieged in. They may feel blocked in being able to go forth in their life, calling, ministry. They may feel helpless regarding a situation or life. They may lose their will to live or have no desire to live. They may feel limited in their ability to progress. They may feel helpless or limited in being able to see or bring forth the promises or prophecies of God. They may feel constantly depleted no matter how hard they try to achieve goals and pursue life endeavors. They may feel defenseless and unprotected against the wiles of the enemy no matter how much they pray, study, fast, or pursue the things of God. They may feel blocked and controlled regarding a relationship or being a part of a group. They may want to leave but the cage has them feeling manipulated, controlled, seduced, bond, where they fear or have a false obligation regarding leaving the relationship or group.

When witches and warlocks infiltrate ministries, they may use cage to siege leaders and ministries in so they cannot discern that they are not of God. The cage causes blockages and blinders where the witches' or warlocks' true motives and identity cannot be detected. It also gives them control over the leader and the ministry where they can manipulate and govern over them for their own personal gain. When caged, saints are manipulated into engaging in ungodly behaviors and practices that bring reproach upon them, the ministry and can even cause them to serve Satan rather than Jesus Christ. The caging demons will oppress leaders and members and have them conflicting with one another in effort to split and destroy ministries, so they cannot be successful in their regional mandate.

Jeremiah 5:25-28 Your iniquities have turned away these things, and your sins have withholden good things from you. For among my people are found wicked men: they lay wait, as he that setteth snares; they set a trap, they catch men. As a cage is full of birds, so are their houses full of deceit: therefore they are become great, and waxen rich. They are waxen fat, they shine: yea, they overpass the deeds of the wicked: they judge not the cause, the cause of the fatherless, yet they prosper; and the right of the needy do they not judge.

Saints who operate through the spirit of Jezebel, Ahab, Athaliah, Goliath, rebellion, rejection, or bewitchment can use their manipulative controlling prayers, false or erred prophecies, demonic or soulish dreams and visions, familiar or ungodly revelations or words of knowledge, demonic or self-willed judgements, and religious acts to cage another saint and/or ministry in. These saints may spend hours praying, days fasting and consecrating, and studying the word, while thinking they are communing with God, but really, they are communing with their own will and/or soul and/or with demons. They then will contend the information they are receiving is from the one true living God, Jesus, and will go on a pursuit to see their word come to pass. The challenge is, they are using religious acts in an erred way which causes those they are pursuing to be caged into their ungodly workings.

Apostle Jackie Green of JGM-Enternational Prayerlife Institute contends that the cage can operate through slanderous words, a demonic incantation of witchcraft workings, and afflictions sent by the principalities and powers of a region that are using the person, witch or warlock to box the leader and the ministry in where they cannot grow or advance the kingdom of God. She believes such a caging is an attack against new ministries or those who are doing a work of overthrowing principalities and powers in a region or territory. The goal is to stifle or destroy the leader or ministry, so they are stuck or die without completing their ordained mandate.

It is also important to note that sometimes the enemy will create situations that run you into a cage. Elijah ran from Jezebel after a powerful showdown where he humiliated her and killed her prophets (Study *1Kings 19-20*). Her threatening words became an incantation to him and SHIFTED him into fear, depression, helplessness, hopelessness, isolation, and suicide. David ran from Saul and from Absalom. He ended up in a cave running from Saul and on top of a mountain running from Absalom (Study *1Samuel 21-24, 2Samuel 12-22*). God had to give Elijah and David strategy for how to get out of their caged situations.

Demons Working in Regional Alliances by Siege Warfare

A person can may also be tracked by the principalities and powers as they travel while going in and out of regions. It doesn't matter if the person is going on vacation, headed to the family reunion, or on a ministry assignment. The person is marked because of the mandate on their lives. The trackers – demonic scouts share information regarding that person with other regions, and the principalities and powers of that region release warfare against that person. The person may overthrow it but by the time they deal with the warfare in one region, info has already been sent ahead to other demon camps in other regions for the purposes of attacking when they enter the next region. The goal is to give no breathing room to adequately rest and refresh from ministry and warfare, and to bring such calamity until the person has no choice but to cease ministry to tend to all the repercussions of warfare or to quit ministry all together. I believe some of the main reasons we have lost some great generals in the faith before their time is because of siege warfare. We are so busy doing the gospel that we have not recognized the fullness of the fight that we are in or do not recognize the strategies we need in different seasons to combat warfare, so we are uncovered, and thus the enemy takes out some who have been critically important to the kingdom of God.

Breaking Demonic and Witchcraft Sieges

There are three critical elements required to loosen and destroy a demonic or witchcraft siege:

1. The breaker anointing,
2. The word of God, and
3. The fire of God.

The combination of those three is a power punch to the enemy that will break every level it has trapped the person, place or thing. The following is a partial list of those levels:

- personally,
- financially,
- relationally,
- economically,
- regionally,
- politically,
- progressively,
- ministerial,
- soulfully (mind, will, emotions).

Micah 2:13 The breaker is come up before them: they have broken up, and have passed through the gate, and are gone out by it: and their king shall pass before them, and the Lord on the head of them.

Isaiah 10:27 It shall come to pass in that day That his burden will be taken away from your shoulder, And his yoke from your neck, And the yoke will be destroyed because of the anointing oil.

Jeremiah 23:9 Does not my word burn like fire?" says the LORD. "Is it not like a mighty hammer that smashes a rock to pieces?

Holman Christian Standard Bible "Is not My word like fire"--this is the LORD's declaration--"and like a hammer that pulverizes rock?

Break the curses and cast out the demons that are holding the cage together.

Galatians 3:13-14 Christ hath redeemed us from the curse of the law, being made a curse for us: for it is written, Cursed is every one that hangeth on a tree: That the blessing of Abraham might come on the Gentiles through Jesus Christ; that we might receive the promise of the Spirit through faith.

Use the blood of Jesus, works of the cross, and name of Jesus to blot (obliterate, wash, wipe) out all ordinances (decrees, prayers, judgements, doctrines) and declare your authority over principalities and powers.

Colossians 2:14-15 Blotting out the handwriting of ordinances that was against us, which was contrary to us, and took it out of the way, nailing it to his cross; And having spoiled principalities and powers, he made a shew of them openly, triumphing over them in it.

Paul and Silas were caged (imprisoned), because of their work for the Lord, and praise and worship broke them out.

Acts 16:25 – 26 About midnight Paul and Silas were praying and singing hymns to God, and the other prisoners were listening to them. Suddenly there was such a violent earthquake that the foundations of the prison were shaken. At once all the prison doors flew open, and everybody's chains came loose.

Praise is a weapon that SHIFTS atmospheres. Praise transforms cages into divine sanctuaries where the kingdom of God manifests in one's midst.

Psalms 100:4 Enter into his gates (heavenlies) with thanksgiving, and into his courts (throne room) with praise (exaltation): be thankful (adoration) unto him and bless his name.

As you praise the gates of heaven are open to you and you are postured inside the court room - the throne room of heaven.

Gates represent access and courts represents judgement and justice being released. Your praise of God and unto God is releasing filling up your life, generations, situations, regions, spheres, nations, climates, frequencies, airways, with the truth of who God is and the truth of his identity is releasing judgment and justice on your behalf.

The power of praise:

- **SHIFTS** out darkness and SHIFTS into the light of God.

- **SHIFTS** out bondage and SHIFTED into the liberty of God.

- **SHIFTS** out the will of man and demons and SHIFTS into the will, purposes and plans of God.

- **SHIFTS** out idolatry and mixture and SHIFTS into the sovereignty and total reverence of our only true and living God - Jesus Christ!

Please note that shifting **out** of something is only half of the objective. It is equally essential that you shift **into** a new place. God becomes sovereign in every situation and sphere concerning us when we praise and since nothing can contend with his sovereignty, it must bow and SHIFT out!

Like Elijah and David, it is essential to also seek God for personal strategies for breaking caging situations. Especially when scouting and warring for others. They may not be aware that they are caged in and may be so bound that they cannot receive truth regarding the cage that is binding them. It will take strategy to break them free and to keep them free.

ASSERTING AUTHORITY IN HEAVENLY REALMS
(Establishing position quickly & precisely in prayer)

The information in this chapter is from my book, *"Embodying A Kingdom Watchman,"* and is in reference to entering the heavenlies quickly and sustaining in your position for the purpose of successful warfare and intercession. A scout cannot adequately operate in their calling if they are not skilled in entering and governing through heavenly realms or assisting others with governing from their divine position of authority.

This prayer strategy is to be used when:

- Initially opening and setting the atmosphere for a service or event.
- Establishing oneself in the heavenlies before engaging in intercession and warfare during one's personal prayer time.
- Establishing a prayer team in the heavenlies before engaging in intersession and spiritual warfare.
- When the atmosphere or heavenlies is blocked and breakthrough is needed so the glory and kingdom of God can enter in.
- Governing in and through heavenly realms.

This manner of prayer is different from just praying to God. When we pursue opening and maintaining an open heaven, combatting forces, and establishing God's kingdom, the enemy counterattacks. He is not willing to give up his territory and will fight and use whatever legal ground available. The enemy will strive to obstruct our prayers and take us out in the process. The enemy is overtaken when using this prayer strategy as you maintain your authority in heavenly realms, and continuously go higher and deeper in the matters and realms of God successfully.

One of the greatest keys to positioning in an authoritative stance that opens the heavenlies is to exalt God.

Exalt is "*rum*" in Hebrew and means:
- To rise, raise, bring up high
- To be lifted up, extol, magnify

The enemy hates when we exalt God. God becomes exponentially huge within the heavenlies as we release adoration unto Him.

1Chronicles 16:28-29 Give unto the Lord, ye kindreds of the people, give unto the Lord glory and strength; Give unto the Lord the glory due unto his name: bring an offering, and come before him: worship the Lord in the beauty of holiness.

When we are crediting the Lord for his glory and strength, we are exalting God in a bold, courageous vigor.

The Amplified Version Ascribe to the Lord, you families of the peoples, ascribe to the Lord glory and strength.

Dictionary.com defines *"ascribe"* as:
- To give credit or assign, as to a cause or source
- Attribute; impute, assign to a source
- Synonyms: accredit, attribute, charge, credit, hang on, lay, pin on, refer, reference

Dictionary.com defines a *"scribe"* as:
- Public clerk or writer
- An author, usually one having official status

A scribe writes and when we write, we make the vision plain. In other words, we establish it. When we exalt God, we are establishing His accreditation within the heavenlies and in and among the people and region. We are writing a decree that He is good and better than all who think they are gods. Our words are being used to literally write in the atmosphere and upon the hearts of people who God is and what His characteristics are toward his people. It affirms the quality of who He is as your God.

The Message Version of verse 28 reads, Splendor and majesty flow out of him, strength and joy fill his place.

The idea that we can give God strength is fascinating. Knowing that we can release exaltation that makes Him even greater and powerful is overwhelming! That's a level of glory and worship many haven't tapped into yet. Our exaltation pushes and drives the devil out of our sphere while releasing the King of glory into our midst. This is a weapon the enemy cannot contend with. The enemy will therefore use an alternate means to find some legal ground to keep his position as the prince of the power of the air-the heavenlies and of this world *(Ephesians 2:2, 2Corinthians 4:4).*

Exaltation is about honor and the best way to release honor is through thanksgiving and praise. When we honor God, we access his gates and his courts. *Psalms 100:4* states that we are to *"Enter into his gates with thanksgiving, and into his courts with praise."* There is no way to get anything out of a place without going through an entry point. Before you can access anything in a room, an office, a vault, the heavenlies, or any other location, you must first enter the space. Whether it is a door, window, or gate, the first requirement is to enter in order to access the goods.

When we come into the presence of one another, we must first enter in. Even on a phone or text, we must go through a process to connect. We physically pick up the phone and dial or text the number. Even if we want something, the polite mannerism (honor) to initially display is to connect with a greeting before we further access our desires or needs.

Prayer is no different. God tells us to enter His gates with thanksgiving and His courts with praise. Gates are literal entry ways within the heavenlies that we go through to access God's kingdom. Courts are where His judgments take place.

The key of thanksgiving allows us to access beyond the gates. The key of praise grants us access into God's courts.

Even when Jesus taught the disciples how to pray, he revealed to them the importance of honor by exalting God.

Matthew 6:9 states After this manner therefore pray ye: Our Father which art in heaven, Hallowed be thy name.

Dictionary.com defines "*hallowed*" as:
- Regarded as holy; venerated; sacred.
- To make holy; sanctify; consecrate.
- To honor as holy; consider sacred; venerate.

Hallowed exalts God as holy and sacred. It displays God's consecrated nature among all the heavenlies. We know where there is holiness, there is light and thus the glistening holiness of God dispels darkness.

The word "*Father*" is a title of honor and with Jesus' words "Our Father," he specifically reveals the object of his prayer. He is not praying to Buddha, Mary or any random idol god. He is specifically acknowledging his holy daddy who is in heaven. Though we do not have to use Jesus' exact words when praying, honor and acknowledgement of God alerts the heavenlies and the demonic realms of who is being glorified. Such exaltation positions us as the authoritarian in the spirit realm. By exalting God, we bypass any legal right for demonic forces to block our prayers.

The Message Version of that scripture states Our Father in heaven, reveal who you are.

This Message Version further confirms that as we exalt our daddy God, we are revealing His nature, character, power, sovereignty, matchlessness, HIS RULE OVER EVERYTHING & EVERYONE! Whewwwwww!

Jesus prayed further, *"Thy kingdom come. Thy will be done in earth, as it is in heaven (Matthew 6:10)."*

The Message Version declares Set the world right; Do what's best––as above, so below.

Jesus is now positioned as the authoritarian among the heavenlies. By stating "thy kingdom come," he calls for a shifting in His sphere of influence so that His surroundings can take on the likeness of the kingdom of God. He is declaring the glory, nature, and character of God's presence to manifest.

One thing I learned about the glory is that it is already around us. The enemy is constantly at work, so the spirit realm and the world tend to look like or mimic his kingdom. It is God's glory that is around us. When we are calling for the kingdom of God to come, we are not just activating and accessing glory from heaven, we are also revealing unconcealed glory that is hidden, lingering or neutralized within the earth and sphere around us.

Isaiah 63:7 And one cried unto another, and said, Holy, holy, holy, is the LORD of hosts: the whole earth is full of his glory.

As we call for the glory, God's presence fills up all around us and our sphere begins to feel and look like the kingdom of God. God begins to "*set the world right,*" such that His standard becomes our earthly and atmospheric standard.

Before conducting spiritual warfare or intercession, we should have already repented for our sins as continual daily repentance takes away the legal ground of the enemy and gives us pure authority to operate as ambassadors in the heavenlies. Sometimes, it is essential to repent again and to repent for the sins of those in our midst, as well as the sins of the region. It is also important to forgive and release forgiveness to debtors.

In Matthew 6:11, Jesus prays Give us this day our daily bread. And forgive us our debts, as we forgive our debtors.

Debts in Greek is *"opheilema"* and means:
- That which is owed a debt. The metaphor is dues: specifically of conjugal duty
- Something owed, such as (figuratively) a due; morally, a fault: debt.
- That which is owed that which is justly or legally due, a debt metaph. offence, sin.

Debtors in Greek is *"opheiletes"* and means:
- One who owes, e.g. person indebted; figuratively, a delinquent; morally, a transgressor (against God): debtor, which owed, sinner.
- One who owes another, a debtor one held by some obligation, bound by some duty.
- One who has not yet made amends to whom he has injured.
- One who owes God penalty or whom God can demand punishment as something due, e.g. a sinner.

This is where the enemy attempts to gain his legal ground. Though not always the case, this is also the reason we will enter the spirit realm or open the heavenlies through praise and worship, but it is as if the glory of God does not abide among us. It will feel like the heavens have closed or our prayers are not penetrating. When this is happening, it is important to explore whether God was sufficiently honored such that we establish our authority in the heavenlies, or whether there is a debt that has not been repented of or forgiven. When God is honored, the heavens will open, and glory will be revealed. However, if repentance or forgiveness is an issue, the enemy will assume we owe him and he will fight us by overtaking the heavenlies and nullifying the effects of the glory so that we think God is not among us or is not responding to our prayers. Repentance of our sins and forgiving our transgressors clears the debts by releasing the redemption of the work of the cross and God's unconditional love against the enemy.

When praying to open the heavenlies for a congregational service or for the purposes of warfare and intercession, repentance and forgiveness must advance to levels of repenting for the transgressions of the region, land, and groups of people.

2Chronicles 7:14 If my people, which are called by my name, shall humble themselves, and pray, and seek my face, and turn from their wicked ways; then will I hear from heaven, and will forgive their sin, and will heal their land.

Generational and corporate repentance and forgiveness is necessary. This clears the legal rights of the enemy and enables the atmosphere or region to remain under God's rule and authority. The Holy Spirit will guide you in whether repentance and forgiveness are necessary and in what areas or issues the repentance is needed. I will list some repentance considerations just to jolt your spirit in this area:

- Repentance for sin within the church as a whole or even the body of Christ.
- Repentance for political decisions made in the community, region, or nation that are contrary to God's law or word.
- Repentance for murder, abortion and ungodly bloodshed.
- Repentance of sins done upon the land to which you are dwelling.
- Repentance for sins of perversion, idolatry, witchcraft, and disobedience.
- Sin against the house of God, gossip, betrayal, murmuring, and complaining.

Jesus prays further in Matthew 5:13 And lead us not into temptation but deliver us from evil: For thine is the kingdom, and the power, and the glory, forever. Amen.

The Message Version Keep us safe from ourselves and the Devil. You're in charge! You can do anything you want! You're ablaze in beauty! Yes. Yes. Yes.

Once we have repented and released forgiveness, deliverance invades which clears our debt and the debt of our debtors and solidifies our established position in the heavenlies. We have exalted God with praise and worship, called for a revealing and outpouring of God's glory, repented and released forgiveness where necessary. We are then safely positioned to proceed into warfare, intercession and/or service plans, as we are inside the gates and courts of God. We have access to the kingdom of God, operate through his power and glory, and can further prevail against the enemy.

The more you implement this prayer strategy, the quicker and easier it will be for you to assert and live through your authority in the heavenlies. SHIFT!

RECEIVING SCOUT INSTRUCTION AT NIGHT

Demonic experiences in your dreams and sleep can be due to sin, witchcraft, generational strongholds and open doors, stuff you watch on tv, what you listen to, open doors to spirits of the dead from your family line, etc. These attacks can also be due to what is occurring in your home with others that live their or visit, what's in your community, region or the environment around you. You have to close up doors to the transgressions and sins in your life and the lives of others. You have to consistently anoint and pray over your home, dedicate and declare your home and life off limits to demons and wickedness, and place a hedge around your life and all that concerns you so you can cut it can be a habitat where God delves and operates.

You can experience dream attacks or demonic visitations due to your calling. Apostles and prophets and those in fivefold offices are called to contend with principalities and powers. Seers, dreamers, intercessors, watchmen, scouts also are called to contend against high ranking demon forces and powers.

Ephesians 6:12 lets us know we will deal with wickedness in high places, so all saints can be subject to demonic encounters in the night. We must understand that our night season is just as important as when we are awake during the day. We must make sure God is governing our night season even as he is Lord of our day and that even though we are resting, we are fortified against the enemy.

Psalms 16:7 I will bless the LORD, who hath given me counsel: my reins also instruct me in the night seasons.

When God gives counsel and instruction at night during our sleep, he is providing advice, instruction, strategy, tools, keys, guidance, insight, foresight regarding his will and purpose for our lives, callings, and regarding those he has granted to our hands. As scouts, we therefore, must SHIFT our minds to expecting to commune with God during the night as we sleep even as we talk and walk with him during the day. Our entire life is a destiny journey with the Lord.

In communing upon our beds, be assured we will endure spiritual warfare during the night and experience spiritual warfare dreams. This is because our spirit is eternal and never sleeps. Our body and soul require rest, but our spirit is active, vibrant, and capable to connect and commune with Lord.

Psalms 121:4-8 Behold, he that keepeth Israel shall neither slumber nor sleep. The Lord is thy keeper: the Lord is thy shade upon thy right hand. The sun shall not smite thee by day, nor the moon by night. The Lord shall preserve thee from all evil: he shall preserve thy soul. The Lord shall preserve thy going out and thy coming in from this time forth, and even for evermore.

God is all spirit. His spirit never slumbers or sleep. We have his spirit in us. Our spirit is always ready, active, awake, and eager to be engaged.

Matthew 26:40-43 And he cometh unto the disciples, and findeth them asleep, and saith unto Peter, What, could ye not watch with me one hour? Watch and pray, that ye enter not into temptation: the spirit indeed is willing, but the flesh is weak. He went away again the second time, and prayed, saying, O my Father, if this cup may not pass away from me, except I drink it, thy will be done. And he came and found them asleep again: for their eyes were heavy.

In *Psalms 77:5-6,* we find David meditating on all God had done through the years. His heart was filled with song and his spirit was awake and active to ponder and explore the depths of the presence and activities of the Lord.

I have considered the days of old, the years of ancient times. I call to remembrance my song in the night: I commune with mine own heart: and my spirit made diligent search.

David was experiencing a form of soaking prayer where he was so caught up in the presence of God that the glory succumbed him and sent his spirit translating into the spirit realm. His spirit was diligently searching the deeper things of God.

As we consider scouting in the night, and how our spirit man is always active, let's take a moment to consider spiritual warfare. Demonic forces wage war with the believers of God in effort to hinder them from:

- Living in the fullness of salvation that Jesus provided through his works and resurrection on the cross.
- Journeying in dominion in the earth, and over the world's and demonic kingdom.
- Believing, proclaiming and drawing souls to Jesus Christ.
- Advancing the kingdom of God.

Ephesians 6:12 For we wrestle not against flesh and blood, but against principalities, against powers, against the rulers of the darkness of this world, against spiritual wickedness in high places.

The Bible tells us that we will experience war and contentions from the enemy.

Matthew 11:12 And from the days of John the Baptist until now the kingdom of heaven suffereth violence, and the violent take it by force.

Often contentions are not legal. That is the reason we must stop saying that people must be in sin if they are experiencing demonic oppression or contention. Spiritual warfare is about authority, territory, and dominion in the earth. The enemy wants to rule people and the earth and is roaming about to fulfill his demonic mandate in the earth.

Spiritual warfare is about authority, territory, and dominion in the earth.

John 10 :10 The thief cometh not, but for to steal, and to kill, and to destroy: I am come that they might have life, and that they might have it more abundantly.

1Peter 5:8 Be sober, be vigilant; because your adversary the devil, as a roaring lion, walketh about, seeking whom he may devour.

Spiritual warfare is the acknowledgement and the engagement of combat. First, you must acknowledge and live your Christian life recognizing that there is a war. Secondly, you must engage in the war and not act like it is just for some believers or only when the enemy is attacking you. It cannot become "situational" warfare where believers contend with and overthrow demonic forces only when it impacts their lives, families, ministries, business, lands, communities, and regions.

Spiritual warfare is an offensive stance against the enemy. You are not defending yourself from the petty wiles of the enemy. You are contending for the right to govern and reign through the kingdom of God in the earth.

Genesis 1:28 was God's plan for man when he created us and the heaven's and the earth, and it was his mandate when he sent Jesus to restore us unto eternal life.

And God blessed them, and God said unto them, Be fruitful, and multiply, and replenish the earth, and subdue it: and have dominion over the fish of the sea, and over the fowl of the air, and over every living thing that moveth upon the earth.

Due to being defensive in counterattacking the enemy, we tend to experience warfare in our lives and dream realm for the following reasons:
- Because we are resting so our guards are down and thus the enemy attacks.

- To instill fear, shame, guilt, affliction, plant seeds of perversion, lust, trauma, tragedy, bewitchment, hardship, murder.
- To cause weariness, tiredness, drainage, restlessness, insomnia, frustration, depression, heaviness, discouragement, hopelessness, helplessness, stress, distress.
- To break our will so we will yield to sin, transgressions, relent our process and progress, become stagnant, and even give up.
- To make us think God does not care and can or protect us.
- So, we will fear the enemy and think he has more power than we have over him.
- To weary, distract, or discombobulate us when we have ministry assignments or life situations on the horizon.
- Bring retaliation or backlash due to ministry assignments or life endeavors.
- Take advantage of open doors due to personal and generational sin or transgressions.
- Attack the calling of God in our lives as many prophets, apostles, Intercessors, and what I call scouts can experience spiritual warfare.
- Release retaliation or backlash due to ministry assignments or life endeavors.
- Take advantage of open doors due to personal and generational sin or transgressions.
- Attack the calling of God on our lives.

A lot of these attacks can be and should be prevented if we as believers posture ourselves offensively. Spiritual warfare is part of our walk and mandate. It will occur and we should be engaging demonic forces in war rather than waiting on them to attack us or waiting on our petty or naturally occurring experiences. When we are "triggered" into getting mad at the devil, that is an exposure of a weakness in our spiritual character and one that the enemy will use again and again.

One result of putting on a spiritual warfare mindset with occurrences or situations is the devil may or may not have anything to do with what happened, resulting in mix of emotional and spiritual response. Without living a life of spiritual warfare and dominion, we become disabled from our destiny to displace and demolish demonic strongholds.

Also, because we do not like or can discern visions, dreams, and even conversations with God that reveal the demonic plans of the enemy, we nullify the strategies, keys, and tools he gives us to defeat the enemy. We say we want to take over regions and set captives free; we want to break the strongholds off our family line and cast out the destiny spirits and familiar spirits, but many do not want to do the work it will take in the spirit realm to stand up to and overthrow demons and their kingdoms.

Even as God sends prophetic dreams and soul-healing dreams, he also sends spiritual warfare dreams. God can invoke spiritual warfare dreams, visions, and encounters to reveal, contend, and displace the assignment of the enemy. He also utilizes spiritual warfare dreams to warn, correct, judge, or turn the hearts of his people from sin, transgression, and the wiles of the enemy.

Job 33:14-18 For God does speak —now one way, now another — though no one perceives it. In a dream, in a vision of the night, when deep sleep falls on people as they slumber in their beds, he may speak in their ears and terrify them with warnings, to turn them from wrongdoing and keep them from pride, to preserve them from the pit, their lives from perishing by the sword.

This type of dream is one we would consider to be a nightmare and of the devil, but the word says that God allows such dreams to terrify the person or the people the dream is for with warnings. When one is in terror, they typically experience intense fear, anxiety, panic, or fright. The dream may be violent or have bloodshed. The dream is unpleasant, and a person may even experience intimidation or coercion. Remember that a terrorist is sent to terrorize. For this reason, it is important to examine dreams with the Lord before automatically assuming it is the devil. I believe this is the reason the Lord tells us in *Psalms 90:5*, not to fear the terror by night as the terror could be the devil, or the terror could be him. Either way, we have authority over the terror if it is the devil and our repentance, closing doors, and turning from sin and transgression, can nullify the acts of the terror coming from the Lord. We have authority through God to understand the meaning and application of the dream.

Psalm 16 (NIV) Keep me safe, my God, for in you I take refuge. 2 I say to the Lord, "You are my Lord; apart from you I have no good thing."3 I say of the holy people who are in the land, "They are the noble ones in whom is all my delight."4 Those who run after other gods will suffer more and more. I will not pour out libations of blood to such gods or take up their names on my lips. 5 Lord, you alone are my portion and my cup; you make my lot secure.6 The boundary lines have fallen for me in pleasant places; surely, I have a delightful inheritance. 7 I will praise the Lord, who counsels me; even at night my heart instructs me. 8 I keep my eyes always on the Lord. With him at my right hand, I will not be shaken.9 Therefore my heart is glad and my tongue rejoices; my body also will rest secure, 10 because you will not abandon me to the realm of the dead, nor will you let your faithful[b] one see decay. 11 You make known to me the path of life; you will fill me with joy in your presence, with eternal pleasures at your right hand.

In *Psalms 16*, David was boasting of the guarding, keeping, and protection of the Lord, and how because he walks in alignment with the Lord, his life experiences the pleasures and inheritances of God's kingdom. He goes on to boast of how he is not like the wicked who serve idols, seek his harm, the harm of God's kingdom, and how God provides him with counsel in the night seasons, meaning,

- During the night,
- During his night meditations,
- In his dreams and night visions,
- And even as he sleeps, to defeat his enemies.

He goes on to declare that this is how he sets God before him - how he is offensive against the enemy.

The word *"set"* is an apostolic word. It is an actual place of authority and dominion - an office - where we reign inside and through the presence and kingdom of God. David further declared that God will not allow him to experience the hell or the corruption of the enemy. He is talking about spiritual warfare. Spiritual warfare is not a flat tire, an alarm failing to go off, somebody giving the finger in traffic. That word corruption means *snare*.

Snare refers to being bound, buried, even possibly destroyed by the enemy. His soul being in hell infers experiencing torment and deadly challenges, though he is not dead but alive. It is about living hell on earth. Because of the counseling encounters of the Lord, David can avoid these attacks and even annihilate them. God shows him the path of life and in God's presence there is fullness of joy; at thy right hand there are pleasures for evermore.

Spiritual warfare dreams, visions, and encounters will sometimes look like nightmares but will possess keys, strategies, and insights to defeat the enemy. They may appear to be nightmares because you may be seeing the inside of spiritual realms or inside the literal camp of the enemy. You may see creatures or creeping things that you have never seen before as the demonic realm is not pleasant. Where do you think the influence of horror movies and gross gruesome music, shows, stories, come from? These writers and directors are encountering dark realms and spheres.

Remember that there are creatures even in heaven. In Revelations, Paul saw four beasts with six wings around the throne worshipping God. They were full of eyes within.

Revelations 4:8 And the four beasts had each of them six wings about him; and they were full of eyes within: and they rest not day and night, saying, Holy, holy, holy, Lord God Almighty, which was, and is, and is to come.

Now before I knew better about dreams and visions, if I would have had this encounter, I would have sworn it was a demonic altar or the beasts were trying to use worship to see into the kingdom of God (laughing but every serious). There are sights and creatures in heaven that we have never seen before. Sometimes many of us have this type of dreams, visions, or encounters and do not realize we are engaging God or heaven. We do not even think to ask God what they mean so they are overlook and devalued.

The devil's camp is hideous; wickedness is evil and horrid. It is a nightmare. I had to ask God to help me to discern when I was really having a nightmare and when I was having a dream that providing intel into the enemy's camp. There were various people in the Bible that had distressing dreams. These dreams provided insight for overcoming during famines and other crises. We have painted such a pretty gospel until we lack true discernment. I do not want to make light of nightmares as the Bible speaks of the terror by night.

Psalms 91:5 Thou shalt not be afraid for the terror by night; nor for the arrow that flieth by day.

Proverbs 3:24-26 When thou liest down, thou shalt not be afraid: yea, thou shalt lie down, and thy sleep shall be sweet. Be not afraid of sudden fear, neither of the desolation of the wicked, when it cometh. For the Lord shall be thy confidence, and shall keep thy foot from being taken.

The word *fear* in this scripture is *"pahad"* which is the same word for terror in Psalms 91. This Hebrew word means, *"sudden alarm, terror, dread, great dread, an object or thing of dread."*

The Amplified Bible When you lie down, you shall not be afraid; yes, you shall lie down, and your sleep shall be sweet. Be not afraid of sudden terror and panic, nor of the stormy blast or the storm and ruin of the wicked when it comes [for you will be guiltless], for the Lord shall be your confidence, firm and strong, and shall keep your foot from being caught [in a trap or some hidden danger].

Nightmares will come to steal our peace and sweet sleep. But we have power over them as they are manifestations of the enemy. I believe God told us not to fear because he knew he would also give us dream and spiritual encounters that appear are nightmares, and we needed to be able to discern between the two so we can act accordingly. When we are in fear, we tend to blame everything on the devil. When that happens, we are discerning through our emotions rather than our spirit. I had to retrain my spirit man not to be afraid of nightmares, and during times I did become initially afraid, I begin to talk myself through my dreams or spiritual encounters so I can SHIFT out of my emotions into my spirit being in control. During my prayer and study time, I would fill my spirit man with scriptures on who I am in God and the authority I had in God. I learned to embrace that everything about God was not all glam and glory as even some of the heavenly creatures and angels can look scary.

I begin to retrain myself to understand that if it was of God, it was for me and if it was not of God, I had authority over it. When I do have nightmares, often, I am able to navigate through them, even where I become the terror. If I am unable to navigate through them, I wake up and pray to counterattack any attack that came against me. I journal the dream whether it is a nightmare, or a dream God gave to me. The prophetic dreams tend to have great strategies and insight to expose and defeat the enemy in day to day situations or in instances where people, ministries and regions need deliverance and breakthrough. The nightmares can also be to our advantage. I learned to embrace that if the enemy is going to attack me, I am going to learn something about him. So, I ask God for insights and keys even in the nightmares. The enemy hates this. Many of my demonic dreams and attacks have ceased as the enemy does not like me embracing my gift or counterattacking.

Scouts are used to discern principalities and powers and spiritual wickedness in high places. *1Corinthians 12:10* mentions the gift of discernment of spirits. Discernment is the ability to "*yield a judicial estimation, distinguish, judge, dispute or discern between good and evil, particularly demonic forces.*" As God increases your discernment, the eyes of your understanding, which is your seer vision - your knowing – your imagination – your mind – your spiritual senses - are heightened and enlightened with glory to discern the darkness and tactics of devils and wickedness in your sphere.

Ephesians 1:18 The eyes of your understanding being enlightened; that ye may know what is the hope of his calling, and what the riches of the glory of his inheritance in the saints.

A scout is the eyes and ears for the army of the Lord. When intel is needed on the enemy, you can maneuver around the enemy's camp or on the battle ground and collect intel. In the Old Testament, scouting was used all the time as a warfare tactic against the enemy. Moses and Joshua sent men to scout out the land. In the New Testament, scouting was used as a tactic to seize Jesus Christ for the purposes of crucifying him.

Deuteronomy 1:22 Then all of you approached me and said, 'Let us send men before us, that they may search out the land for us, and bring back to us word of the way by which we should go up and the cities which we shall enter.'

Numbers 13:1-2 And the Lord spoke to Moses, saying, "Send men to spy out the land of Canaan, which I am giving to the children of Israel; from each tribe of their fathers you shall send a man, every one a leader among them."

Joshua 7:2 New International Bible Joshua sent some of his men from Jericho to spy out the town of Ai, east of Bethel, near Beth-aven.

Luke 20:20-22 So they watched Him, and sent spies who pretended to be righteous, in order that they might catch Him in some statement, so that they could deliver Him to the rule and the authority of the governor. They questioned Him, saying, "Teacher, we know that You speak and teach correctly, and You are not partial to any, but teach the way of God in truth. "Is it lawful for us to pay taxes to Caesar, or not?"

The devil roams about spying out people and the land seeking whom he can devour.

Galatians 2:3-5 The Message Bible Significantly, Titus, non-Jewish though he was, was not required to be circumcised. While we were in conference, we were infiltrated by spies pretending to be Christians, who slipped in to find out just how free true Christians are. Their ulterior motive was to reduce us to their brand of servitude. We didn't give them the time of day. We were determined to preserve the truth of the Message for you.

Many scouts have dreams where they are conversing with governmental officials, kings, queens, and people with high rankings and platforms. It is important to understand that dreams realms are real. There are territories and spheres of influence just like the regions and platforms we endeavor in our natural lives. Though you may think it is just a dream, some of these encounters may very well be occurring in the spirit realm. God could have translated you as you slept to deliver a message to these officials. God could also be showing you your governmental jurisdiction in the spirit and the natural realm, while posturing you to begin interceding so he can manifest this encounter whether through spiritual translation or through the natural encounters. God could be giving you inside revelation on the heart, intent, and plans of an official for purposes of confounding demonic plans.

Many in the church tend to share these dreams, but rarely do they pray into them, to acquire God's direction concerning them. Many do not know that they should, or how to adequately govern their gift of dreams, so they do not recognize if they had a true encounter or a dream that needs to be interpreted and prayed over for further instruction. Many like to boast about having dreams but that is all they do - BOAST! They never SHIFT to operating in the fullness of the gift because they remain in awe, rather than becoming a governor with the dream realm where they can make an impact in the kingdom of God and the earth.

Often, we take these dreams for granted because we do not believe we will encounter such high-ranking officials. We see ourselves as small people who could never have the opportunity to speak to a king, governmental official, a famous person, or person of influence. Throughout the Bible, kings and governmental officials had dreams and needed the interpretation of "normal everyday people" to interpret them.

Some of these kings and governors were not even believers of the true God, but God spoke to them via dreams. Many of them needed godly people to interpret what was being spoken. Your night visitation to a high-ranking official could be for the purposes of interpreting a dream or word from the Lord that they already received, or to provide further counsel and wisdom regarding that word. You must open your spiritual understanding where God is taken out of your limited box and expanded into the supernatural where he lives and reigns.

God spoke to King Abimelech in a dream to warn him of a death of judgment should he touch Abrahams wife Sarah (Genesis 20:1-8).

Joseph interpreted King Pharoah's dream and was placed over all of Egypt to govern through a seven-year famine (Genesis 41).

King Nebuchadnezzar had dreams that troubled him. His magicians and sorcerers could not interpret the dreams. Daniel was called upon to answer the dreams and in doing so, he gained great favor with the king (Daniel 2).

God appeared to King Solomon in a dream and told him to ask what he wished. He was able to ask for wisdom to govern his reign (1Kings 3:4-15). God gave him that plus riches and honor.

A man appeared to Paul in a dream and told him to come to Macedonia and help them (Acts 16:9).

Pilates wife had a troubling dream warning them not to kill Jesus. She told her husband but because the people were adamant about crucifying Jesus, they chose him over another guilty prisoner even though he was a righteous man and had done nothing to warrant death (Matthew 27:19-23).

God speaks to who he wants and who needs it the most. God uses who he desires to help get his word to people. He is always striving to give messages to those who impact large bodies of people, regions, nations, and the world at large. Often, he speaks to them in dreams, visions, or night encounters. I believe he does this so they cannot deny that it is him speaking. I also believe he does this because many in such positions can yield pride, succumb to being self-focused or self-absorbed in their agenda, do not generally have or adhere to godly wise counsel, or they are surrounded by troops and agents that prevent most who have wisdom, directions, and warnings from being able to relay Godly messages to them. God therefore uses the dream and supernatural realms to convey his messages such that the official knows they received a word from the Lord, and there are consequences to not following his word.

Being translated in the spirit is a biblical act. Many saints contend they desire to engage in such supernatural endeavors, but do not pursue it or posture themselves to experience it. From a young age, my spirit would automatically astral project into the spirit realm when I was sleep. I would encounter all kinds of witches, warlocks, soul travelers, astral projectors, and demons. Often, I was attacked because they would see the light of God around me. They would also follow me back to my home and further attack me in my sleep or visit me on different nights and attack me. I would have all kinds of demonic attacks as I would try to sleep and experience demonic agents and dream killers in my dream realms. All while having these encounters, God would give me powerful insight in the demonic realm and how to assist people and ministries to war against demonic strongholds.

I would also have dreams that would normally equate to nightmares, but inside these dreams, were keys and strategies for defeating the enemy. I would use this information to help ministries, people, and regions be free of demonic oppression and possession. Despite all the wisdom I did receive, because I was not aware of how to handle the demonic attacks or know that what was happening was a gift, I did not understand who I was encountering in the spirit realm and what to do with them, I did not understand the reason I was being attacked, I did not understand that these realms belong to me and I had authority in them, or how to govern my spirit so that I would not be automatically ejected from my body without the leading of the Holy Spirit; I wanted all this to CEASE. Because I did not have understanding, I dreaded this gift and spent half my young adult life trying to stop it from happening.

No one in my church circles, nor at conferences, trainings and events, could help me understand what was occurring, and often I was made to feel like I was in sin, had open doors, dabbling in witchcraft and demonically oppressed for having such encounters. It was not until I was about 37 years old, I am 46 now, that I came across a minister who told me that there was nothing wrong with me, that this was a gift, and I needed to seek God concerning how to control my spirit man and govern this gift so I could operate sufficiently in these realms.

There are many people in the Bible that translated in the spirit realm. The main person everyone speaks of is Paul and how he was given a thorn in his side to keep him humble as he had numerous revelations and supernatural translations in the spirit realm (*2Corinthians 2*). We also tend to hear about Ezekiel and his grandiose dreams, visions, and teleporting experiences (*Ezekiel 8*). It is obvious that Elijah the Prophet teleported in the spirit a lot. So much so that when he left the earth, he was caught up in the spirit right in front of his successor, Elisha, and was seen no more.

2Kings 2:11-12 And it came to pass, as they still went on, and talked, that, behold, there appeared a chariot of fire, and horses of fire, and parted them both asunder; and Elijah went up by a whirlwind into heaven. And Elisha saw it, and he cried, My father, my father, the chariot of Israel, and the horsemen thereof. And he saw him no more: and he took hold of his own clothes, and rent them in two pieces.

Elijah did not even have a burial. He was simply translated into heaven by a whirlwind. Anyone jealous????

In this next passage of scripture, we see Elijah's servant afraid to deliver a word to King Ahab because he feared, Elijah would teleport and go missing in action.

IKings 18:10-13 As the Lord thy God liveth, there is no nation or kingdom, whither my lord hath not sent to seek thee: and when they said, He is not there; he took an oath of the kingdom and nation, that they found thee not. And now thou sayest, Go, tell thy lord, Behold, Elijah is here. And it shall come to pass, as soon as I am gone from thee, that the Spirit of the Lord shall carry thee whither I know not; and so when I come and tell Ahab, and he cannot find thee, he shall slay me: but I thy servant fear the Lord from my youth.

We can discern through the dialog in this scripture, that the Holy Spirit translated Elijah often. He traveled by the spirit just as he did in the natural.

In *John 6*, the disciples rowed their boat several miles away from shore, and Jesus came walking on water. Now in my opinion, either Jesus was walking fast, or he had to be teleported by the Holy Spirit to where they were. Once Jesus entered boat with them, it supernaturally reached its destination. Read it for yourself.

Verse 16-21 The Amplified Bible When evening came, His disciples went down to the sea, And they took a boat and were going across the sea to Capernaum. It was now dark, and still Jesus had not [yet] come back to them. Meanwhile, the sea was getting rough and rising high because of a great and violent wind that was blowing. [However] when they had rowed three or four miles, they saw Jesus walking on the sea and approaching the boat. And they were afraid (terrified). But Jesus said to them, It is I; be not afraid! [I AM; stop being frightened!]. Then they were quite willing and glad for Him to come into the boat. And now the boat went at once to the land they had steered toward. [And immediately they reached the shore toward which they had been slowly making their way.]

That is quite interesting isn't it???? We hear about Jesus walking on water, but no one talks about the boat SHIFTING to shore immediately. That part is often overlooked. But Jesus was obviously consumed by the supernatural power of God to defy time, space, and the natural realm.

In *Acts 8:38-40*, Phillip was caught up in the spirit right in front of a eunuch and was translated to other regions where he was preaching the gospel of Jesus Christ.

And he commanded the chariot to stand still: and they went down both into the water, both Philip and the eunuch; and he baptized him. And when they were come up out of the water, the Spirit of the Lord caught away Philip, that the eunuch saw him no more: and he went on his way rejoicing. But Philip was found at Azotus: and passing through he preached in all the cities, till he came to Caesarea.

Though these experiences and more are in the Bible, we rarely endeavor teachings on how to govern in these realms. Much of these gifts and encounters tend to be associated with witchcraft and though saints contend they want to do greater works than Jesus, and they are supernatural beings, many of the realms of the heavenlies and even in the earth lack the governmental rule of

God's people, which allows demons to take up residents in spheres where we should have influence and jurisdiction. My desire is to give you wisdom so you can embrace dreams and spiritual translation as part of your inheritance and utilize it as a scout in God's kingdom. I decree you will SHIFT in your scout anointing to effectively impacting governments, and political arenas, regions, and nations, while advancing the kingdom of God in the earth and the heavenlies.

Wisdom Tools I Learned Regarding Governing Dreams and Spiritual Realms

- I accepted being a scout as part of my calling. I stopped dreading that though we are all called to overthrow demons. I was called to spiritual warfare dimensions that most would never encounter or understand.
- I stopped trying to make people understand and accept it.
- I stopped trying to make people validate it when they did not understand it or shunned it.
- I stopped waiting on people to train me in it.
- I stopped waiting on people to give me permission to operate in it.
- I stopped waiting on people to get a clue about dealing with demons of this caliber and grasped that it was my gift and calling and a realm of the spirit realm that God has given me authority. I experience warfare and encountering these spheres regardless of others people acknowledgement.
- I had to stopped being angry about what others did not know and see and asserted my right to overthrow darkness and free them and me of anything that was hindering the fullness of our salvation from manifesting. I had to be okay that as I contended in these spheres, especially in different services and events that I attend, and even just when around people - in their homes and the like, that others received credit for ministry that they had/have no clue I conducted in the spirit realm. They think it is their preaching and the like that displaced darkness, broke open the heavens and set

the captive free, but at times, it could be myself and other scouts engaging in warfare that is unbeknownst to those around us that is bringing the breakthrough.

- I decree you are SHIFTING to accepting the full cup of your calling as a scout. SHIFT!

I became offensive in operating in this part of my calling by asking Holy Spirit to show me my identity and my authority in the spirit realm - to teach me the purpose of it, the reason I was called to be a scout, an intercessor, watchman on the wall and to fight principalities and powers. I allowed Holy Spirit to teach me how to stand in the gap, watch and intercede, go into the spirit realm and war and fight to displace principalities, powers, spiritual wickedness in high places, go into the enemies camp and scout out the land.

You must teach your spirit man how to engage in your dreams and in the spiritual realm during prayer and when you are asleep. Since my dreams and encounters were a gift and was not going to stop, I had to learn to be offensive. The Lord revealed to me that even as he is a spirit and never sleeps or slumber, I am more of a spiritual being that anything, and my spirit man is always awake. Like him, my spirit never sleeps, and I had power to engage my surroundings, atmosphere, to engage him, to engage my dreams, and to operate in the spirit through my spirit man. I began to verbally declare this revelation every night before I went to bed. I would declare that though I would sleep soundly, my spirit man was awake and was equipped to discern demonic spirits, witches, and any spiritual entity that entered my space. I declared that I would be able to participate in my dreams and discern demonic attacks and navigate through my dreams victoriously. I spoke that I when I entered the spirit realm, I had authority over all the power of the enemy and was equipped to tread and tower over all darkness through the empowerment of the Holy Spirit. I also closed all generational doors to my spirit illegally and denounced astral projecting in the spirit realm while declaring I would only enter the spirit realm by the leading of the Holy Spirit.

During my prayer and study time, I would fill myself with warfare scriptures and study scriptures and books on dreams, translating in the spiritual realm, deliverance ministry, and spiritual warfare. I would often study books from Christians in Africa and other nations where the supernatural realm was viewed as natural and where these encounters were expected and embraced. Though their experiences were more extreme than mines, I understood that America's demons are rooted more in our culture and trends than many people having supernatural encounters. I do believe this will change as the years progress, especially as people from other nations become citizens in America. We need to understand that as people come, their generational mindsets, strongholds, demons, etc. come with them. The saints truly need to prepare for how the spiritual climate of America will change as the world continues to enmesh culturally and ethnically, but that is a whole other topic, so I digress.

As I declared nightly, and postured myself offensively, I would immediately discern when a demon or witch entered my room. I would wake up and deal with it accordingly. I could navigate and talk myself through my dreams, and have the ability to change my dreams where I was fighting the enemy in my dreams, avoiding impending dangers, and even waking up if there were shape-shifting demons in my dreams that would appear as one thing then change as another and try to attack me, or if my dreams were demonic encounters with demons trying to attack me. If the Holy Spirit translated me into the spirit, I could engage in spiritual warfare, eavesdrop on the enemy's camp and obtain intel, fight witches and warlocks, and conduct ministry as the Holy Spirit led me to various locations. In times past, I would not know what to do, and would often remain suspended in the spirit realm until something attacked me. I dreaded this because it was often a dark, quiet, eerie space. But as I learned that I was actually supposed to be going somewhere, I became engaged with "*Let's go, Holy Spirit,*" and he would translate me where I needed to be, or I would soar through the spirit to where I needed to go. I would acquire intel on the enemy and became more skilled in deliverance ministry and spiritual warfare, where I am able to break people, regions, and ministries, free of specific demonic influences.

During prayer, I often enter translations through soaking prayer. I soak myself in the blood of Jesus and cleanse myself of anything that will hinder me from connecting to God. I then soak myself in the supernatural power of God. I often focus on being translated to the foot of Jesus, the throne room of God, or inside the heart of God. Often, I am translated to these places and if God desires me to translate to other places, he will guide me there and reveal his assignment so I can fulfill it. There are times where I am engaged in spiritual warfare and intercession, and God will translate me in the spirit to do warfare from heavenly places. He may also have me engage principalities and powers, witches or warlocks, or wicked people. Sometimes he will give me a strategy ahead of time and other times he leads me as I pray.

Ask God to teach you how to navigate through your spirit. Please know a consistent prayer and fasting lifestyle is essential to living through your spirit. Your flesh and emotions must die, and you have to continuously seek personal deliverance and healing, so you have nothing in common with demons and wickedness. Repenting quickly, forgiving quickly, and living unoffendable must be your character and lifestyle. Guarding your eye, ear, mouth, heart, and soul gates is essential as demons are always looking for an avenue to gain authority over you. If you have open doors to sin and witchcraft, you risk being attacked rather than journeying victorious in your dream, sleep, and spiritual realms.

I became offensive by learning to accept that fear was a part of life, but I did not have to be fearful. I begin to build myself up in the truth about the power and authority I had over demonic forces and begin to practice living a lifestyle of being courageous and knowing I was victorious over every demon and every life challenge. I stopped fearing devils, the demonic realm and the unknown, and gained clarity and truth about how they feared me. You cannot be afraid to engage dream and supernatural realms. You must live and embody the following scripture, *And Jesus came and spake unto them, saying, All power is given unto me in heaven and in earth (Matthew 28:28).*

It is your right and inheritance to govern in both realms. There are realms and galaxies that we still don't know. We have jurisdiction in these realms. Our spirit man never sleeps; therefore, we should be able to operate in both realms while asleep and awake. However, we tend to encounter heavenly realms more in prayer and in the night when our flesh, soul, and emotions, are postured at rest and reverence to God, such that our spirit realm can truly be led and guided by the Holy Spirit. Imagine how powerful we would be, if we humbled ourselves in this manner when we are awake, such that we could continuously operate through the full power of our spirit? Grow us, Jesus. You cannot be afraid of demons. no matter what size or rank. *Luke 10:19 Behold, I give unto you power to tread on serpents and scorpions, and over all the power of the enemy: and nothing shall by any means hurt you.* I know people say you are not equipped to fight principalities and powers, and I do agree that you should not go picking a fight without strategy. But if you are going to operate in supernatural realms you are going to run into some ugly, hideous, horrifying, humongous, high ranking principalities, powers, territorial spirits, demonic agents, heavenly creatures, angels that are not so glorious looking, and on and on. Ask God to give you confidence to embrace your inheritance of having power in heaven and in earth and practice having a lifestyle totally surrendered to Jesus, where he can grant you access to travel and govern in earthly and heavenly realms.

You cannot be afraid of demons, no matter what size or rank.

I stop waiting on demons and witches to attack me. I learned what attacks me and what attacks the people, lands, regions, and spheres I govern. I became offensive by scouting in prayer through intercession and warfare to overthrow demonic forces and wickedness. I asked God to enlighten me to discern, see, and understand when I was dealing with a demon, witch, warlock, a thrill-seeking person, astral projection and on and on. I learned what attacks and how they attack so I could engage accordingly, judge accordingly, and annihilate accordingly. Ask God to teach you the difference and to give you Godly boldness engage and overthrow demonic and wicked enemies.

Sex Demons - There are all types of sex demons that attack at night besides incubus and succubus. Incubus and succubus are sex demons that enter your sphere or dream realm and have sex with you while you are sleep.

Night Terrors or Nightmare Demons - Spirits of terror or mare attack with fear, suffocation, nightmare dreams, or attack with things that go bump in the night. Children encounter a lot of these spirits as they hide in closets, under beds, behind curtains, on window ledges or around the window area, doorways. Some of these spirits will grow up with children as they become play mates, and spirit guides. Night terrors are often accompanied by unexplainable high fevers in children. It is important not to automatically dismiss a sudden onset of physical symptoms as "it will pass." Typically, the child will wake up as they are being terrorized by seeing the demonic forces that are in the room with them. A parent's counterattack is to anoint with oil, plead the blood of Jesus, hold their child, and offer assurance of protection. A child who experiences night terrors is usually one with the calling of a scout on their life.

Ghost Entities - Sometimes ghost type entities move stuff around a person's home at night and may even attack sexually at night. These entities could be people that have astral projected themselves into the spirit realm and enter people's homes, buildings, and lands, for play, thrill seeking experiences, and sexual games. They like to scare people or take advantage of them while they are resting or sleep. It is my experience that some ghost entities are either people who have died but have not entered heaven or hell or are demons that have taken on human looking bodies. They tend to haunt buildings, lands, or enter peoples' homes and disturb their sleep at night. These ghost entities and family spirits sometimes hang out at movie and entertainment sites, covens, high places, homes and businesses of high priest, witches, psychics, yoga instructors, and work with them in fulfilling demonic schemes and assignments.

Astral Projectors – Witches, warlocks, or regular people who separate their soul from their physical bodies so they can travel around the heavenly realms. Though demons can attack you sexually at night, sometimes these attacks are astral projectors. They are real people translating themselves into the spirit realm to rape and molest people. They do this for thrills or just because, or to feed an altar or satanic power. Sometimes, when people have encounters in their home where they see shadows, figures of people, or things moving around, these are not always what we call ghosts or demonic entities. Astral Projectors love to scare and play tricks on people. They are thrill seekers at the expense of the general public.

As you become keener in discernment, and being interactive in your dreams, you will be able to discern whether you are dealing with demons or astral projectors. Most astral projectors will flee if you threaten to cut their silver cord. The cord is what connects their soul to their body, and they can literally die if they are disconnected from it. They also flee from rebukes in Jesus name and the blood of Jesus. If they do not respond to a rebuke or threat of cutting their cord, they are most likely a ghost entity, or a territorial spirit that has some connection to that region, sphere, land, building, home, etc. This would require a cleansing of the land and building to rid of these attacks.

As an example, The Insane Clown Posse is a music group that unleashed a wave of astral projection onto its followers. Their brand of hardcore hip hop is known as horrorcore and is based on mythology and traveling into death. Their music has a consistent theme of the supernatural and darkness. That is just one example of how secular music can be a gateway to a cultic following by encouraging rebellion against all authority.

Ecclesiastes 12:5-7 Also when they shall be afraid of that which is high, and fears shall be in the way, and the almond tree shall flourish, and the grasshopper shall be a burden, and desire shall fail: because man goeth to his long home, and the mourners go about the streets: Or ever the silver cord be loosed, or the golden bowl be broken, or the pitcher be broken at the fountain, or the wheel broken at the cistern. Then shall the dust return to the earth as it was: and the spirit shall return unto God who gave it.

Demons cannot hold you if you rest in the peace and protection of God. Sometimes when attacked, I begin focusing on resting and being fortified in God's peace. This SHIFTS me out of the grips of the enemy and into the presence of God. *Psalms 91* is a key scripture for asserting your authority of peace and protection.

John 14:27 Peace I leave with you, my peace I give unto you: not as the world giveth, give I unto you. Let not your heart be troubled, neither let it be afraid.

Shapeshifters – Are demons that can change their form to appear as any person living, dead, or fictional. Initially, shapeshifters appear harmless (cats turning into lions and attacking) or even look like someone you know. It will then turn into a demon or evil thing in the dream and attack you. Shapeshifters are often subtle in dreams and tend to attack once they get you to a place of trusting them or thinking you are safe and have no reason to be alarmed. Be discerning as shapeshifters will attempt to draw you to places in a dream where you will be harmed, attacked, or suddenly you are being chased and running for your life.

Familiar Spirits – These are family spirits that go from one generation to the next, attaching to children and wounded people, while living in around their lives. They may become spiritual guides, pose as God or angels, but are really demons who control and direct the person's life. These spirits often lead people on pathways that are not their ordained destiny or that tie them to demonic covenants and vows where they owe Satan for their fame and fortune. Such spirits are the catalysts for curses, cycles, and ungodly patterns consistently operating in family lineages. Familiar spirits are the most common particularly when someone has lost someone they love and become locked into the grieving process. A familiar spirit takes on that person's image, initially offering comfort but ending in multiple negative consequences.

Familiar Spirits that work in dreams and visions look like someone you know, but really are demons. Though familiar spirits will look and sound familiar, they will not have the character or personality of the person you know, will not act the way the person would normally act. They will try to get you to do things that are contrary to God or to what is for you and will not be for you in the dream. Some could be witches and warlocks who engage in these practices to plant demonic seeds and spells or collect items and specimens from their victims so they can use them on demonic altars as a point of contact to prey on them. Sex and blood are two of the strongest gateways witches and warlocks operate through to increase in demonic powers. As demons thrive one perversion and lusts to strengthen themselves with power as sex and blood are forms of life source. Sex allows you to reproduce and blood has cells that enable you to live. Both are potent with power which is the reason witches and warlocks engage in a lot of perverse acts and drink blood. The more they are infused with them the more they are inundated with perverse demonic power as they are using sex and blood for idolatrous means and not for what God intended which is the breed life and give life.

Jesus shed his innocent blood so we could be cleansed of sins and restored unto eternal life. Blood has power to deliver the entire world. Demons knows this. Witches and warlocks know this. Sex carries the ability to procreate and reproduce after its own kind. Demons know that. Witches and warlocks know that. That is the reason they want to make the world perverse and to even kill God's way to have sex and procreate so we can stop producing after God's identity and likeness and produce after the devil's identity and likeness.

Witch (female sorceress) - Warlock (male sorcerer) – As a scout, you will run into witches and warlocks because they live and travel in these realms. Witches and warlocks tend to release their spells and attacks in the night. They use translation and astral projection to enter the heavenlies to work their spells and bind people. You may encounter a witch or warlock when God leads you to go into the heavenlies to intercede and pray. Witches and warlocks will immediately attack you when they see you. They are territorial and will attempt to assert authority over their sphere of influence. They will see the light of God in you and assume you are there to judge them or overtake their sphere. They will attack in effort to protect themselves. Some witches and warlocks will repent and even give their life to God. Some will be sold out to the devil and will stand their ground and fight. Ask God to lead you in how to deal with witches and warlocks.

God may have you cast them out of the heavenlies. God may have you physically fight them. God may tell you to have them repent and give their life to Him as He may want to use them for the kingdom. God may tell you to have them decide whether they choose to repent or die as in the Bible God has little tolerance for witches and warlocks – *"Exodus 2:18 18 Thou shalt not suffer a witch to live."* Some witches and warlocks are sold out for Satan and will choose death because they will refuse to repent. Be sensitive to what God is leading you to do and do not be afraid - for greater is God's power in you than in them.

Some demons will come and attack you because they know the calling on your life. These attacks can start at a young age or begin to occur when you give your life to God or start to walk in ministry. They can increase as you grow in your walk with God, especially if you are doing ministry without clarity of the demonic spirits comparable to the level of ministry you are doing. They will also increase if you are doing ministry with no understanding of your authority. The increase will continue if you assume demonic attacks just come with the territory and you do not become offensive in dealing with demonic forces.

Attacks can also increase in certain seasons of ministry, due to where you are doing the ministry or when you are doing the ministry. If you are one who is prone to night attacks, it is essential to know about the demonic principalities and powers that operate in your region and even seek God for this revelation regarding regions you are going to minister too.

Sometimes God may be giving you revelation and insight about your region, assignments or events you are having or attending through dreams or by allowing demonic forces to visit and reveal themselves to you. It is important when you have these experiences that you search them out and see what God is saying. If he does not give you any information, then pray against what you saw and experienced in the dream. Also pray against whatever spirit revealed itself to you. Do not ignore these experiences as doing so will make your event and assignment difficult when you go forth in what God is saying. Sometimes demonic forces will visit you to intimidate you, instill fear, affliction, harass and distract you, and even to kill you so you can be unsuccessful in fulfilling the assignment God is granting to your hands.

You must embrace your dream realm as a gift and learn to govern it properly. It is not just to share cool dreams, go to heaven, or soar and translate through the spirit realm. You have a work to do whether sleep or awake. There are manifestations in the spirit that we need in the earth realm. Many people that have jurisdiction in dream and spiritual realms are able to go to heaven and bring things to earth, go to the enemy's camp and get things that was stolen, cancel demonic plots and plans, acquire intel on the enemy and use it to beat down him and his kingdom. Many encounters we have with people in our dreams are often real translations. We have to ask the Holy Spirit if it was a real encounter or what to do to bring the encounter to past.

We need these divine connections and interactions to affect government, laws, and ungodly plans in the earth. We also need them to complete ministry assignments and produce miracles, signs, and wonders in the earth. Some of us may never physically go to a foreign country. And though we have internet access, many of us have jurisdiction in foreign countries via the spirit realm that we never utilize. We reject prophetic words revealing this jurisdiction and we are apathetic in our sleep where we do not engage them in our dreams, night season, and prayer time. It is time to arise and take our rightful place in the kingdom. Many of us are too mature to not be fully thriving in the fullness of our destiny and calling. We are adequate, we are trained, and we are equipped. And even more important the Holy Spirit is available to provide hands on teaching and revelation regarding every gift and spiritual endeavor God grants to our hands. Develop a relationship with the Holy Spirit so he can mature you in this gift. He knows all things and is eager to show you the highways of heaven and your authority in every sphere and over the enemy.

✓ Praying for your leader holds them up as they win the battle on the behalf of the kingdom and for us.

✓ Praying for you leader keeps all those under their government safe and overcoming, as the victories of God are released through them and those connected to them.

When praying for a minister, cover the following:

Personally - Their strength, stamina, endurance, physical and spiritual ability to carry the weight of their calling, continual refreshing throughout their assignment, that as they pour out they will be refilled with virtue, that their mantle and anointing would manifest with raw power and limitless measure, that they carry God's divine mandate in their mouth, hands, feet, spirit, and heart to produce his will in the earth.

Loved Ones & Belongings - Their marriage, children, family, their household, ministries, businesses, finances, life situations.

Travel Partners - Those that will be traveling with them - cover their lives, marriage, children, family, their household, ministries, businesses, finances; life situations, that they have a self-sacrificing servants heart and are keen in the spirit to guard, protect, and thwart demonic assignments, messiness, and dangers seen and unseen.

Travel - Use scriptures (e.g. Psalms 91) to release divine hedges of protection; decree that they go in undetected as a sniper or stealth bomber, that their scent, sound, and imprints be erased such that tracker and watcher spirits, destiny killing and familiar spirits, and demonic witches and warlocks cannot pick them up in the realm of the spirit. Pray for safety on planes, in cars, hotels, and events. Cancel all spiritual and natural terrorist attacks against their lives, destiny and calling.

Angelic Assistance - Release angels to travel with them, cover them in their dream and sleep realm, to go before them to cultivate a heavenly atmosphere, bring heaven to earth, to encamp around about the service, to assist with ministry, to push back, war and dismantle demonic kingdoms, principalities and powers that would oppose the Lord's work, to intervene on demonic assignments, to complete specific assignments connected to the event at hand.

Their Food and Health - This is a huge one as food tends to be the love language of Christendom. Food does not have the nutritional value it once did, and it is easy to eat whatever is put before you when you are being hosted by people. Ministers do not like to cause offense or dishonor yet there is minimal regard for providing foods that replenish the body, that digest well after a late-night service, or that keep ministers healthy. It is highly beneficial for ministers to use supplements or essential oils to offset nutritional malnourishment and let host ministries know what meals are best for them. This is one of the ways infirmity and disease is taking our ministers and we need to take responsibility to CHANGE this dynamic. Witches and warlocks release spells upon ministers' foods to cause discomfort and affliction where they are distracted and bound - unable to effectively focus on ministry. Pray for wisdom on what foods to eat and not to eat, where and when to eat, and break demonic ingestion, curses, spells, and hexes off foods and beverages.

Night Season - Declare a blood, fire, and glory wall to encamp around about their place of rest; use the blood of Jesus to pray for a cleansing of all demonic, sin, dedications, and curses that have been released in or around the atmosphere of the place the minister is staying, pray for demonic and witchcraft portals to be closed up in their sleep and dream realm; pray that unauthorized demonic visitations are off limits and send angels to deal with all night tares, telepathy, witches, warlocks, astral projectors, and night agents. Cancel all demonic deposits and attacks that would try come through the dream and soulish realm and decree only divine dream and throne room encounters occur as they sleep and rest.

MINISTER PRAYER COVERING

When we cover our leaders, it lessens and dismantles our warfare and tribulation. This is because the anointing flows from the head down, so when our leaders are strong and able to adequately lead us, it keeps us protected under the government and authority of God that is on their lives.

> **Psalms 133:3** *It is like the precious ointment upon the head, that ran down upon the beard, even Aaron's beard: that went down to the skirts of his garments.*

The government of God flows through the precious ointment – anointing oil - that mantles the leader. A mantle is an assigned power that God's called believers are covered, enveloped, and conceal with.

<u>Ointment</u> in the Greek is "*semen*," and means:
- *grease, especially liquid (as from the olive, often perfumed) figuratively, richness*

- *anointing, fatness, fruitful, oil((-ed)), ointment, olive, pine*

- *medicament (healing substance, medicine, remedy) or unguent for anointing (balm or salve for wounds, sores, etc.)*

- *fat (things or of fruitful land, valleys)*

As we are properly aligned with our leaders, covenanting and journeying in life with them, receiving and flowing in ministry and destiny vision with them, submitted to their authority, the anointing that is on their lives runs down to us, as we are the body to which the skirts of their mantled garments are covering.

> *1Corinthians 12-14 For as the body is one, and hath many members, and all the members of that one body, being*

many, are one body: so also is Christ. For by one Spirit are we all baptized into one body, whether we be Jews or Gentiles, whether we be bond or free; and have been all made to drink into one Spirit. For the body is not one member, but many.

Their anointing provides reenforcement of our salvation as we become part of the body to which they govern. We are thus reinforced in our deliverance, healing, protection, refuge, prosperity, posterity, etc., as we are covered through the authority that is on their lives.

When you are praying for your leader, you are holding up their hands such that we all prevail.

Exodus 17:9-13 And Moses said unto Joshua, Choose us out men, and go out, fight with Amalek: to morrow I will stand on the top of the hill with the rod of God in mine hand. So Joshua did as Moses had said to him, and fought with Amalek: and Moses, Aaron, and Hur went up to the top of the hill. And it came to pass, when Moses held up his hand, that Israel prevailed: and when he let down his hand, Amalek prevailed. But Moses' hands were heavy; and they took a stone, and put it under him, and he sat thereon; and Aaron and Hur stayed up his hands, the one on the one side, and the other on the other side; and his hands were steady until the going down of the sun. And Joshua discomfited Amalek and his people with the edge of the sword.

- ✓ Praying for your leader keeps them from succumbing to weariness in the battle – their spirit is willing but their physical body may get weak at times. Your prayers strengthens their bodies, minds, and souls.

- ✓ Praying for your leader keeps them fortified as they submit to God and advance his will and purpose in the earth.

Nullify Lashings - Break the powers of backlash, front lash, side lash, lash from heavenlies, witches, warlocks, spiritual wickedness in high places, hell, the grave and the underworld.

Prayer Results

The person, ministry, business, etc. you are praying for should:

- Know what to expect and can be offensive against the enemy and with their ministry assignment.
- Minimal to no warfare or the ability to endure or tower over it without consequences.
- Can ignite revival and regional reformation as the region is impacted by what is released through the event.
- A closing - hedging in.
- More peace, joy, and fulfillment of their calling and assignments.
- Less to no concern about family, loved ones, ministry and business endeavors.
- Not worried or fearful of retaliation and backlash.
- Able to focus and produce effective ministry with signs following.
- Can multitask and complete other assignments.
- No sleep attacks and unauthorized demonic visitations.
- Labor less yet experience great breakthrough.
- More supernatural stamina and strength.
- Quicker recovery from ministry.

SPIRITUAL MAPPING

Spiritual Mapping of The Region

- Seek Holy Spirit for knowledge of the main principalities, powers, idolatries, witchcraft, worldliness, and perversions that control a region. Combat, cast out, displace, and cleanse these areas as he leads and cancel any way, they would impact.
- Seek Holy Spirit as well as use Google to acquire information from geographical and historical studies of the region and pray into or against what God reveals to you through that information.
- If you are in or near the region, drive around and receive information via Holy Spirit and pray from what is shared.
- Repent for the generational sins done in the region.
- Repent for the sins of the ministry and the people that will attend the event.
- Break up the fallow ground by repenting for the sins done in the land of the region; remove all curses, demonic covenants, strongholds, demonic squatters, watchers, foot soldiers, and other demons that have overtaken the land.
- Repent for witchcraft done in the region and upon the land and for blood, human, and idolatrous sacrifices offered to Satan.
- Break the powers of brass heavens and inconsistent open heavens, command an open heaven over the region not just the service. You want what God will do to impact the region not just the service.

Spiritual Mapping of the Service

- Pray for the glory and kingdom of heaven to overtake the venue and become the literal throne room of God.

- Ask God to show you what is in the people, ministry, and atmosphere as far as demonic strongholds, sins, bondages and begin breaking these off them.
- Ask God to show you the principalities and powers impacting the venue, people, ministry, and the event and utilize the strategy he gives you to overthrow this. Share this information with your scout leaders so that they can have others pray and contend with you.
- Pray for conviction, true repentance, a contrite and broken spirit, a desire for transformation to reign in the people, ministry, and atmosphere.
- Pray for demons to be exposed and cast out, and for the very word, worship and ministry to be so judgmental and tormenting that it drives them out.
- Pray that demonic assignments to be immediately discerned and thwarted.
- Pray that any demonic and witchcraft assignments being sent against the minister be thwarted.
- Pray that the Holy Spirit is liberated to move freely in the service.
- Expect that authentic praise and worship will reign in the service.
- Pray that revival fire and revival reformation is stirred in the people, ministry, and atmosphere such that what is imparted is eternally ignited to SHIFT the people, ministry, and atmosphere further into the purposes and vision of God long after the minister has left the region.
- Pray that the glory is tangible and lacks restriction to be unveiled in the earth and poured out without measure so the creative and demonstrative power of God can flow.
- Pray believing that deliverance, healing, breakthrough, miracles, signs, wonders flow.
- Pray for the gifts to freely flow and produce the identity and fruit of God.

I want to encourage you to practice discerning principalities and powers and even scouting so that you can see into the demonic realm and spiritual realms as natural as you do the earthly realm. Though this is a gift I did not ask for and have had from childhood, I have taught my team how to scout out the land, and they are able to keenly discern principalities and powers.

Keys to Embracing Principalities and Powers

- Embrace spiritual realms as part of your calling (Ephesians 2:6, 1Corinthians 2:14).
- Possess a desire to see and discern demonic forces (Hebrews 4:12, Matthew 10:16).
- Ask God for the eyes of your understanding to be enlightened to discern demonic forces, especially those in your region and sphere of influence (Ephesians 1:8).
- Live a life of daily deliverance so you can be alert and combative against demonic infiltration (Matthew 15:26, Romans 12:2, Psalms 34:19-21).
- Know and exercise your authority over all demonic strongholds (Luke 10:19, Hebrews 5:14).
- Utilize your faith to ascend and live in and from the third heaven, above principalities and powers, so you can contend from your rightful place of authority in God (Ephesians 2:6).
- Want and possess your inheritance of lands and spheres within spiritual realms, as we have land and spheres that are due us in the spiritual realm even as we do in the natural (Ephesians 1:3).
- Have a desire to judge principalities and powers and to see them overthrown (John 7:24, 1Kings 3:9, 1Thessalonians 5:21).
- Possess a heart to see God's kingdom reign in the earth (Matthew 6:10, Matthew 11:12, Luke 11:20).

- Assert your authority concerning your right to see and discern the schemes of the enemy (1Peter 5:8).

Decreeing you are SHIFTING even more in being an efficient scout as you invest in your position and become this revelation!

SHIFT FORTH! SHIFT!

EVENT PRAYER COVERING

Pre-Event Individual and Team Prayer

If there is a team of people chosen to pray for a minister and to cover an event, I recommend them coming early (30-60 minutes early) and gathering before a service to pray collectively. You come early because a scout is always on his or her post ahead of time. You come early to position yourself to effectively complete your assignment. After praying, I recommend the person, or the team walk throughout the event grounds inside and out to pray over the event. Even if this is an event where the minister is a guest preacher, you can get permission to do this, or you can do this quietly by praying as you walk the grounds. Sometimes what hinders breakthrough is what has not been dealt with in the land where an event is taking place. Dealing with sin issues, demonic dedications, vows, and covenants, removing watcher spirits, squatter spirits, scanner spirits, ease dropping spirits, demonic agents, and foot soldiers is effective in seeing breakthrough for people and a region. Often the glory is hovering in the atmosphere but has not penetrated the land or the essence of the people, so people are touched but transformation does not occur. As the ground is healed and tilled, the atmosphere is more pliable to receive the glory of God.

Pray the Following for the Event
- Exalt Jesus and establish his kingdom and authority.
- The Heavens to be open.
- Fallow ground to be broken up.
- Remove all scanner, watcher, scatter spirits, ease dropping spirits, foot soldiers, and demonic agents.
- Repent for past and present sins, and dedicate the ground, atmosphere and region to Jesus.
- Declare enmity by nullifying anyway the principalities and powers would try to demonically stronghold or influence the ground, atmosphere, event, minister, and the people.
- Release angels to contend with principalities and powers.

- Contend against all witchcraft attacks and manifestations and deal with spiritual wickedness that is demonically strong-holding or influencing the ground, atmosphere, event, minister, and the people.
- Call for the Holy Spirit to come and be liberated.
- Call for an outpouring of glory, revival fire and dunamis power.
- Pray anything other specific detail that God gives.

Pray the Following for the Minister

- Supernatural health and for any afflictions and illnesses to cease.
- Supernatural strength and endurance.
- Blessings and favor with heaven, the region, and with the people where they can be welcomed and received even if having to minister a controversial or hard word.
- Demonic and witchcraft attacks and assignment to the impeded.
- Any hinderances, conflicts, confusion, and drama to cease.
- Shielding inside the blood, fire, and glory of the Lord so they can be protected during ministry.
- Glory to be radiating and cultivating.
- Anointing to be strong, tangible, penetrating, transforming.
- The preached word to be clear, revelatory, piercing, while dividing of soul and spirit, convicting, and liberating.
- Revival reformation to be tangible and transferable.
- Immediate refilling of the virtue of God.
- Canceling of backlash, side lash, front lash, lashes from hell. This is especially important to pray after the service has ended.
- Pray anything else God gives to you.

Praying During the Service or Event

It is important to operate from heavenly realms when covering a minister and an atmosphere for an event. By faith, you want to enter in the spheres above the service so you can peer down into the service from a keen posture of what is occurring in the service and in and around the minister that is covered by your prayer. This should already be your life posture as *Ephesians 2:6* contends that we are seated in heavenly places in Christ Jesus.

And hath raised us up together and made us sit together in heavenly places in Christ Jesus.

Since this is a finished work after the cross, the word *set* denotes an eternal place - an eternal authority and governing in God - an established seat of authority inside the heavenly realms in Christ. As you posture yourself to live from this place, you begin to understand that you are not of this world and govern through the kingdom of heaven. One way to learn to live from your seated posture is to *"Set your affection (mind) on things above, not on things on the earth (Colossians 3:2)."*

> *You are not of this world and govern through the kingdom of heaven.*

Affection in Greek is *phroneō* and means:

- to exercise the mind, i.e. entertain or have a sentiment or opinion
- by implication, to be (mentally) disposed (more or less earnestly in a certain direction)
- intensively, to interest oneself in (with concern or obedience)
- set the affection on, (be) care(-ful), (be like, be of one, be of the same, let this) mind(-ed), regard, savour, think

Set is a finite focus and position where you are seeking to be, think, do, speak, like Jesus, seeming you are sitting inside of him. Every time life, circumstances, people, demons, try to get you to view life or focus on earthly things, you have a spiritual mandate to posture your thoughts, feelings, perceptions, and considerations on things which are godly and kingdom minded. To simplify, have you ever heard an adult tell a child to sit up straight? That is because slumping is not healthy! When you shift from the earth realm to the spirit realm, it is a divine version of "Sit up straight!"

The criteria for what being godly and heavenly minded can be found the following scriptures.

Philippians 4:8 Finally, brethren, whatsoever things are true, whatsoever things are honest, whatsoever things are just, whatsoever things are pure, whatsoever things are lovely, whatsoever things are of good report; if there be any virtue, and if there be any praise, think on these things.

Romans 12:2 And be not conformed to this world: but be ye transformed by the renewing of your mind, that ye may prove what is that good, and acceptable, and perfect, will of God.

John 4:34 Jesus saith unto them, my meat is to do the will of him that sent me, and to finish his work.

John 8:29 And he that sent me is with me: The Father hath not left me alone; for I do always those things that please him.

As you PRACTICE and LIVE through this posture, it literally becomes your identity. You will find that while physically raising you up above the earth and earthly matters, you are able to discern, strategize, provide solutions and results from a heavenly perspective.

As you are in a service interceding for a minister and the event, you are in this posture. You are therefore able to discern the truth of what is occurring in the service and how to pray to cover the minister. You should be able to detect:

- Whether God is present.
- If the heavens are opened or closed.
- If the enemy is trying to close the heavens or snuff out the move of God.
- If religion and tradition need to be broken or the people and the Holy Spirit can freely flow.
- If the ground is hard and need to be plowed and broken up.
- What is of God and what is not.
- Whether angelic activity is in the room.
- Whether demons, witches and warlocks are in the room and need to be bound, cast out, or overthrown.
- Whether a mixture or the pure glory of God is in the room.
- If the people are bound or free and areas of needed deliverance.
- What needs to be prayed to bring breakthrough.
- If there is disorder or confusion in the room.
- If repentance is needed to make the atmosphere, ground and people pliable for God to move.
- If demonic or witchcraft attacks are occurring against the minister or the service and warring to break them.
- What weapons, fruit of the spirit, gifts of the spirit, attribute of the anointing (e.g. deliverance, healing, miracle, dunamis power, breakthrough, liberty, etc.) the minister needs from God and the kingdom of heaven to fulfill his or her assignment, and to pray it into the atmosphere.
- Contend for the full purpose of God to manifest in a service.
- Do not stop praying until the service has ended.
- After the service, an eternal solidification of all that occurred.

As God reveals matters to you, you pray accordingly. When necessary, it would also be beneficial to communicate some information that is of a serious nature with your team so you all can unify in prayer. If you are not sitting together then this can be done through the great technology of text message.

THE POWER OF PRAYER AGREEMENT

It is important to examine the power of prayer agreement as scouts. Unity is a weapon that gives us keen advantage over demonic forces and wickedness. When we pray together, we become a violent army taking the kingdom by force. Prayer is the most advanced weapon we have in our arsenal. It fits any time and is effective in any season.

Matthew 11:12 And from the days of John the Baptist until now the kingdom of heaven suffereth violence, and the violent take it by force.

An army works together. They are on one accord in:

1. Mind (perception and understanding - thoughts and feelings)
2. Heart (the heart is where our treasure is - importance and value)
3. Soul (focus and attention - target, posture and disposition)
4. Action (behaviors - roles, duties performance, acts, deeds, encounters, engagements)

Such unity produces the will, purpose, miracles, signs, wonders, government and atmosphere of the kingdom.

Below are a few scriptures that operate in our fellowship and unity of the faith:

Philippians 2:1-2 The Amplified Bible So by whatever [appeal to you there is in our mutual dwelling in Christ, by whatever] strengthening and consoling and encouraging [our relationship] in Him [affords], by whatever persuasive incentive there is in love, by whatever participation in the [Holy] Spirit [we share], and by whatever depth of affection and compassionate sympathy, fill up and complete my joy by living in harmony and being of the same mind and one in purpose, having the same love, being in full accord and of one harmonious mind and intention.

1Corinthians 1:10 Now I exhort you, brethren, by the name of our Lord Jesus Christ, that you all agree and that there be no divisions among you, but that you be made complete in the same mind and in the same judgment.

Romans 15:5 Now may the God who gives perseverance and encouragement grant you to be of the same mind with one another according to Christ Jesus.

Acts 5:12 At the hands of the apostles many signs and wonders were taking place among the people; and they were all with one accord in Solomon's portico.

Acts 8:6 The crowds with one accord were giving attention to what was said by Philip, as they heard and saw the signs which he was performing.

Romans 12:16 Be of the same mind toward one another; do not be haughty in mind, but associate with the lowly Do not be wise in your own estimation.

Philippians 1:27 Only conduct yourselves in a manner worthy of the gospel of Christ, so that whether I come and see you or remain absent, I will hear of you that you are standing firm in one spirit, with one mind striving together for the faith of the gospel.

There are powerful manifestations of the Lord and his kingdom that occur when we agree in prayer together.

Matthew 18:19-20 Again I say unto you, That if two of you shall agree on earth as touching any thing that they shall ask, it shall be done for them of my Father which is in heaven. For where two or three are gathered together in my name, there am I in the midst of them.

The Amplified Bible Again I tell you, if two of you on earth agree (harmonize together, make a symphony together) about whatever [anything and everything] they may ask, it will come to pass and be done for them by My Father in heaven. For wherever two or three are gathered (drawn together as My followers) in (into) My name, there I AM in the midst of them.

When we are agreeing together, we are on one accord regarding:

- Who we are praying to (Our father which art in heaven).
- What we are praying for (Your kingdom come, your will be done on earth as it is in heaven).
- What we desire from God (Give us this day our daily bread. And forgive us our debts, as we also have forgiven our debtors. And lead us not into temptation, but deliver us from the evil one).
- Making sure the fullness of the kingdom manifests (For thine is the kingdom, the power and the glory, for ever and ever. Amen).

Agreement is vitally important because prayers are atmospheric. Generally, we like to have a whole lot of people praying for us. We tend to think the more people praying, the more the kingdom of God is bombarded to hear and answer our prayers. What we do not take into consideration is everyone does not pray the same. People tend to pray through their own perception of what you are asking them to pray for and may not be praying exactly what you believe they should be praying concerning your situation. This causes different opinions and perceptions regarding your prayers to be released into the atmosphere on your behalf. If God has spoken a promise or prophecy regarding you, then the prayers that are speaking contrary to what God has said, could be the very resistance and delay that is causing your prayers not to be answered in the timing that you need them.

The word tells us to guard our words because they have power to curse or to bless (*Proverbs 18:21, James 3:10, Proverbs 15:4, Ephesians 4:29*). Once words are released, they live on the frequencies, airways and heavenlies around us. Science has proven that sound is an eternal experience. It continues outwardly forever and ever. *Revelation 5:8 "And when he had taken the book, the four beasts and four and twenty elders fell down before the Lamb, having every one of them harps and golden vials full of odors, which are the prayers of the saints."* Our prayers are kept in the heavenlies and have a fragrance!

Prayers are petitions so they are not just words, they serve as applications for a court order or for some judicial action. In a court of law, it is good to have credible witnesses who can verify and agree with what you are saying. A witness can make or break a case. A witness can sway, prolong, delay, or stifle a case. A witness that is not properly vetted can say something that could give the prosecution leverage over you. This is the reason lawyers prepare even the best witness before putting them on the stand. The lawyer will make sure the witness can handle themselves in court and then will take them through a series of court scenarios to make sure they are ready for the contention and battle of court. If a witness is not found to be ready, then often they are not used. A lawyer may not allow the person whose trial it is to take the stand for this reason. If they are not good under pressure, are not ready to stand their ground, cannot properly convey their stance, then they will not be used in their own court case. Do you see how important this becomes? This is the reason *Ephesians 6:11 tells us to "Put on the whole armour of God, that ye may be able to stand against the wiles of the devil."* We must be properly vetted with salvation, truth, faith, righteousness, the gospel of peace to stand and assert our authority over the enemy.

Your Facebook audience may not be properly vetted. The 2,000 strangers you expose your petitions to, may not be properly vetted. Your family and friends whose salvation is hanging on by a thread, may not be properly vetted. Those church folks who pray the nice prayers and do not believe in deliverance and warfare, may not be properly vetted. These are just points for provoking exploration as we all have a right to pray. We all have a right to petition the throne of grace (*Hebrews 5*). But we do want to make sure we are petitioning with bold agreement that incites a heavenly response of judgement, justice, favor and blessing. Though we do pray publicly, prayer is a private matter between the petitioner and the Lord. Numbers lessen intimacy. It also does not equate to a quick victorious response. This is the reason I believe Jesus said the following:

Matthew 6:5-6 New International Bible And when you pray, do not be like the hypocrites, for they love to pray standing in the synagogues and on the street corners to be seen by others. Truly I tell you, they have received their reward in full. But when you pray, go into your room, close the door and pray to your Father, who is unseen. Then your Father, who sees what is done in secret, will reward you.

- Prayer is intimate.
- The throne room and courtrooms of heaven are intimate.
- Our prayer petitions are intimate and are meant to be handled with care.
- The dynamics of prayer, even the contending of it is intimate, sensitive, and strategic; it is not a show to display our talent, promise, or need, nor for everyone to participate.

We know from the scripture that Satan roams about, showing up for heavenly and earthly court.

Job 1:5-7 Now there was a day when the sons (the angels) of God came to present themselves before the Lord, and Satan (the adversary and accuser) also came among them. And the Lord said to Satan, From where did you come? Then Satan answered the Lord, From going to and fro on the earth and from walking up and down on it.

Since he is a roamer, he and his imps can show up at anytime and anywhere to contend against you and your prayers. You want witnesses and petitioners that can stand their ground against him and his kingdom to overthrow his workings. Some people mean well but may not be able to stand and pray to the dimension to which you need covering or breakthrough.   Jesus experienced this with his own disciples.

Matthew 26:36-41 Then cometh Jesus with them unto a place called Gethsemane, and saith unto the disciples, Sit ye here, while I go and pray yonder. And he took with him Peter and the two sons of Zebedee, and began to be sorrowful and very heavy. Then saith he unto them, My soul is exceeding sorrowful, even unto death: tarry ye here, and watch with me. And he went a little further, and fell on his face, and prayed, saying, O my Father, if it be possible, let this cup pass from me: nevertheless not as I will, but as thou wilt. And he cometh unto the disciples, and findeth them asleep, and saith unto Peter, What, could ye not watch with me one hour? Watch and pray, that ye enter not into temptation: the spirit indeed is willing, but the flesh is weak.

These disciples were Jesus' closes confidants, his inner circle, yet in this time of his life, though willing, they were not able to sufficiently pray and cover him. Though Jesus kept seeking the disciples for prayer, he had to contend alone during one of the most difficult battles of his life. This example demonstrates that prayer is delicate and nothing about it is to be taken lightly. Even who we seek prayer from in certain seasons of our lives is just as important as the prayer petition itself.

Though these hand-picked disciples were Jesus' closest confidants who loved him and walked with him, when it came time to stand against the wiles of the enemy, they crumbled. They either denied or watched silently as Jesus was persecuted. They had already demonstrated this weakness during intercessory time, so it is understandable that they would manifest it during the natural battle. When I consider this biblical example, it baffles me how people can post their prayer petitions online and expose their intimate courtroom sessions with strangers. It baffles me how folks can have a prayer group of hundreds and thousands of folks but many of them are strangers who are not given specific direction on how and what to pray. It baffles me how we ask some folks for prayer, knowing they are living two lives, in sin, mentally unstable, dabble in witchcraft, ill equipped, unequally yoked as it relates to beliefs. The disciples were none of these things. They were trained by the best - Jesus himself - yet they were not equipped for this courtroom battle. They were willing but their flesh was weak. Therefore, their consecration of the flesh was not in agreement with the dimension of prayer Jesus needed at that time.

> ". . . their consecration of the flesh was not in agreement with the dimension of prayer (Jesus) needed at that time."

Relationship and fellowship with the person, ministry and vision you are praying for strengthens the power and results of prayer. Jesus had personal relationship with the disciples, so he had expectations of them being able to support him, cover him and pray with him. In this instance, his expectation was for them to labor with him for one hour. He knew their gifts, callings, abilities and potential. This is the reason he rebuked them when they kept falling asleep. And this was the reason he knew it was their flesh, not their spirit and not their love for him that was not consecrated to pray with stamina. He was able to grant them grace due to knowing them and even give them revelation on where they needed to grow so that temptation would not overtake them.

Though we are always open to pray for others, and God will give us his burden to labor for someone or something, it is very difficult to labor in prayer for someone you do not know. The exception is when God gives someone a prayer assignment of which is comparable to him depositing his heart in them for that matter. Otherwise, people often lack tenacity, fervency, consistency and focus to labor in prayer with someone they do not personally know. When God gives a prayer assignment, the person is usually praying from a posture of obedience as it relates to duties and position. This is the reason *James 5:14-16 says, "Is any sick among you? let him call for the elders of the church; and let them pray over him, anointing him with oil in the name of the Lord."* The elders will labor through their position as it is their duty to pray but even then, it will take building relationship for fervent, consistent prayer to occur. As a scout, I love to pray and will take on various prayer assignments as God leads, but it has been relationship that has led me into fervent laborious prayers.

People need to know what warfare they are pairing to when connecting to your vision.

Romans 15:30-31 Now I urge you, brethren, by our Lord Jesus Christ and by the love of the Spirit, to strive together with me in your prayers to God for me, that I may be rescued from those who are disobedient in Judea, and that my service for Jerusalem may prove acceptable to the saints.

New International Bible I urge you, brothers and sisters, by our Lord Jesus Christ and by the love of the Spirit, to join me in my struggle by praying to God for me. Pray that I may be kept safe from the unbelievers in Judea and that the contribution I take to Jerusalem may be favorably received by the Lord's people there, so that I may come to you with joy, by God's will, and in your company be refreshed.

Paul was letting the brethren know that by praying for them, they were joining his struggle. They had now become companions of the ministry he was doing, what would happen to him as he ministered, and the spiritual battle that was occurring as he completed the work of the Lord. He regarded it as "striving" with him. Striving is a military word for it denotes that we are at odds or at war. When we are striving,

- We are exerting ourselves vigorously.
- We are working hard and strenuously in achieving our desired purpose and goals.

- We are contending in opposition, battle, competition and conflict with our opponent.
- We are battling – rivaling – any resistance against our fate.

Paul gave clarity about what he was doing and the prayer assignment for the believers. This provided strategy regarding who the enemy was and how to combat him. Often, we tell people to pray, yet, there is no revelation of what we are striving to accomplish. When no strategic prayer requests are given to a group or team, it leaves them vulnerable on the battleground because they are not able to come together as a military prayer unit in specifically contending against their target. People are susceptible to backlash because they are praying blindly or made to figure it out with God on their own. If God does not speak on the matter, then the people are left to pray from their perceptions or tap into witchcraft psychic behaviors in effort to pray for the matter at hand. Some people are quick to make these blind prayer requests spiritual by saying, "*Just pray for me; God will lead you.*" If you really trust someone to pray for you then you should not be secretive about your prayer need. If you do not trust them, or the prayer request is too intimate to share then you should not be asking them to pray, as prayer is strategic and personal. It is also a striving war and everyone cannot strive with you, will not strive with you, and cannot handle the opposition that you endure; especially if you are not providing strategy to guide them in sufficiently covering and contending for you.

We need to stop this irresponsible madness. I decree a SHIFT RIGHT NOW! SHIFT! There is power to agreeing and being on one accord in prayer and in seeking to procure God in the earth. SHIFT!

Acts 2:1-9 And when the day of Pentecost was fully come, they were all with one accord in one place. And suddenly there came a sound from heaven as of a rushing mighty wind, and it filled all the house where they were sitting. And there appeared unto them cloven tongues like as of fire, and it sat upon each of them. And they were all filled with the Holy Ghost, and began to speak with other tongues, as the Spirit gave them utterance. And there were dwelling at Jerusalem Jews, devout men, out of every nation under heaven. Now when this was noised abroad, the multitude came together, and were confounded, because that every man heard them speak in his own language. And they were all amazed and marvelled, saying one to another, Behold, are not all these which speak Galilaeans? And how hear we every man in our own tongue, wherein we were born?

Accord is *homothymadon* in Greek and means:

- unanimously: — with one accord (mind).
- with one mind, with one accord, with one passion.
- A unique Greek word, used 10 of its 12 New Testament occurrences in the Book of Acts, helps us understand the uniqueness of the Christian community.
- *Homothumadon* is a compound of two words meaning to "rush along" and "in unison."

The image is almost musical; several notes are sounded which, while different, harmonize in pitch and tone. As the instruments of a great concert under the direction of a concert master, so the Holy Spirit blends together the lives of members of Christ's church.

They were on one accord and in one place. Despite being from different cultures, ethnicities, nationalities, discourses, they were able to unite unanimously and experience one of the most profound movements of the Holy Spirit that impacts Christendom to this day. This is a vital key for prayer teams and scouts collaborating to cover leaders and ministries. We are God's spiritual beings that possess his nature, character, principles and fruit. We thus, can unite in his likeness and demonstratively SHIFT forth his kingdom in our midst where are impacted despite differences in identity.

Due to the advancement of technology, sometimes we are not in one place in the natural but must unite in one place – heavenly places in the spirit – so we can be and operate on one accord. This is vital when praying over the internet and phone lines. We are in different atmospheres and different locations. We must take authority over the realms and spheres of everyone who is praying, bind them together under the governance of God, SHIFT together into our rightful place in heavenlies, then begin praying our prayer focus. When we fail to do this, we encounter a lot of disruptions and interferences as principalities, territorial spirits and powers combat our prayers and disrupt their effectiveness. The internet and phone lines are atmospheric, so witches and warlocks also navigate in these spheres. They have cohorts such as watcher spirits, squatter spirits, tracker spirits, demonic agents, ease dropping spirits working for them; gaining intel so they can release assignments to hinder the progress of saints. There is godly sovereign power in unity. We need to close inside of it, take authority over these realms and spheres, and close off the wiles of the enemy and his imps so that we are praying inside the secret place of God; on one accord in heavenly places, governing with all authority through him.

The questioning warfare that came after this experience could not strip the power of this historical Holy Ghost filled moment. It has stood the test of time. It has become a prayer catalyst for waiting on God and being baptized in his spirit by fire. Let us take note that all the inquiries came from outsiders and came after the experience. This was an intimate space of seeking and waiting on God. For Jesus had told them to wait in expectation for the Holy Spirit would surely come with power.

Luke 24:49 And behold, I am sending the promise of My Father upon you. But remain in the city until you have been clothed with power from on high."

Acts 1:8 And, being assembled together with them, commanded them that they should not depart from Jerusalem, but wait for the promise of the Father, which, saith he, ye have heard of me.

It was an intimate space of intercession and warfare. Even as they were assembled - WAITING - they were striving together. They were being conscious of being in one place, focus, posture and purpose together so they could receive the promised victory of the Holy Spirit. This is the power of agreeing in prayer. The sovereign will and intent of the Lord manifests when we are committed and clear in vision about what we are doing for him. I decree that a SHIFT comes to the body of Christ, where we become visionary military scouts. Strategically implementing the principles of God so that his kingdom can tangibly manifest in the earth. MAY HIS SHIFT EMBODY YOU NOW IN JESUS NAME! SHIFT!

RESOURCES

Books by Taquetta Baker
Apostolic Mantle
Embodying A Kingdom Watchman
Sustaining the Vision Workbook
The Great Awakening: Igniting Regional Revival

Book by Apostle Jackie Green
Church Planters Spiritual Warfare Manual

Online Reference Sources
Blueletterbible.com
Biblestudytools.com
Dictionary.com
Olivetree.com
Strong's Exhaustive Bible Concordance Online Bible Study Tools

Photography and Editorial Team
Cover photo vision by Tashema Davis, Owner of Echo Gallery

Editorial Team:
Amanda Latrice, Nina Cook, and Dr. Kathy Williams

You can link with me or any of my support team through Facebook.
Connecting with me will give you access to each one on the team.

---

www.ingramcontent.com/pod-product-compliance
Lightning Source LLC
Chambersburg PA
CBHW051832040426
42447CB00006B/497